Living Fear Free

Living Fear Free

Overcoming Agoraphobia—The
Anxiety/Panic Syndrome

Melvin D. Green

A former agoraphobic who has helped hundreds
achieve RECOVERY

Kendall/Hunt
Publishing Company
Dubuque, Iowa

Printed in the United States of America

B   403668   01

I wish to dedicate this book to my wife Rosemary who stuck with me through the agony of agoraphobia, and for her love, assistance and patience during the year I took to write this book.

Contents

The author was agoraphobic for 35 years of his life. In this chapter, he describes his life as an agoraphobic . . . his pain, frustration and anger . . . from early childhood through his adult years . . . and on to RECOVERY.

The *TRUE* definition of agoraphobia is presented in lay terms. The reader attains new insights into the problem and comes to the realization that agoraphobia is not a mental condition, but a series of life experiences that can be changed. Case histories are presented and a special section is included for physicians and other professionals to help them identify and diagnose the agoraphobic.

Why does a person become agoraphobic? How does it begin? Who can be affected? This section fully explains the various conditions and experiences that can create agoraphobia. Agoraphobia must be understood before it can be dealt with.

In this chapter we examine the physical symptoms commonly experienced by agoraphobics and how to deal with them. A basic understanding of the nervous system and the principles involved in controlling unwanted physical responses are included.

An in-depth look into the agoraphobic personality. Why are agoraphobics so hard on themselves? How can they handle the frustrations of agoraphobia? How do they relate to other people who do not understand what they are experiencing? These and many more questions are answered.

Chapter 6: Giving Yourself Permission to Be Human and Imperfect, 55

Agoraphobics are perfectionists. They do not allow themselves to be less than perfect in many areas of their lives. This chapter explains the fallacy of perfectionism and how it keeps the agoraphobic limited. Techniques to change this behavior are included.

Chapter 7: Negative Anticipation, **69**

Negative anticipation is the most destructive and limiting of all the agoraphobic traits. The reasons the agoraphobic is constantly dealing with the "what if's" are discussed and explained. Techniques to change the negative anticipation to positive experiences are included.

Chapter 8: Confidence and Self Esteem, **77**

In this chapter we discuss two necessary and important adjustments an agoraphobic must make in order to attain recovery. Why low self esteem and lack of confidence is a part of the agoraphobic personality is explained. How to attain more confidence and self esteem, become more assertive, overcome fear of rejection and criticism and other vital subjects are covered.

Chapter 9: Fear and Risk, **83**

The agoraphobic is always feeling fearful . . . fear of an impending panic attack . . . fear of an upcoming event . . . fear of what others might think or say . . . fear of life. The reasons for these feelings and how to overcome them are discussed.

In order to attain recovery, the agoraphobic must take risks. Techniques to get past the fear and take the risks are explained.

Chapter 10: Anger, **91**

Suppressed anger is extremely detrimental to those suffering from agoraphobia. If the anger is not dealt with, anxiety and stress increase. How it can be dispelled safely and permanently are discussed.

Chapter 11: The Fearful Child, **97**

Will your child become agoraphobic? What signs to look for and how to prevent future agoraphobia is discussed. School phobia and how it relates to the agoraphobic personality is explained.

Chapter 12: The Female Agoraphobic, **105**

Statistically there are more female agoraphobics than men. Reasons for this and the sociological role of the female is explained. The agoraphobic wife and mother is discussed and problems pertaining to them are solved.

Chapter 13: The Male Agoraphobic, **111**

The male agoraphobic has problems dealing with the created limitations and fears that may not be part of the female agoraphobic's lifestyle. The author has intimate and personal knowledge of these problems, since he was a male agoraphobic. These problems and solutions are discussed. Case histories are included.

Chapter 14: The Functional Agoraphobic, **119**

Contrary to popular thought, the homebound agoraphobic is the minority. Most agoraphobics are functional, although their movements be limited. Techniques on how to expand your "safe place," be less dependent on others and grow from functional to recovered are discussed.

Chapter 15: The Homebound Agoraphobic, **123**

What fear can be so great as to create a prison out of your own home? Why is this "adjustment" perfectly "normal"? How do you prepare to walk through the door to freedom? These questions and many more are answered.

Chapter 16: The Support Person, Family and Friends, **127**

"No one understands me." This is the cry of the agoraphobic. In this chapter, agoraphobics learn how to communicate their feelings and needs to those around them. The attitudes of the support person, family and friends are discussed so that better understanding can be attained by all involved.

Chapter 17: Drugs, Alcohol and Nutrition, **133**

Some agoraphobics use drugs and alcohol extensively to reduce the feelings of anxiety. The most commonly used drugs and the side effects are listed. The tendency towards alcoholism by agoraphobics and how to avoid it is discussed. Your diet and how it can affect your emotions are also covered.

Chapter 18: The Meaning of Recovery, **145**

Many agoraphobics do not understand, or are fearful of, recovery. In some cases the fear of recovery may be greater than the pain of agoraphobia. The "true" meaning of recovery and overcoming the fear is discussed. Case histories are included.

Chapter 19: Taking Charge of Your Life, **153**

Taking charge of your own life . . . that is what recovery is all about. How to lead a normal life without the anxieties and symptoms of agoraphobia are discussed. Case histories are included.

Chapter 20: Kathy's Story—From Homebound to Recovery, **161**

Kathy is a classic agoraphobic. Her personal life story from childhood to being totally unlimited is outlined. It is both touching and inspirational and should be read by all agoraphobics.

Cross Index, **171**

By using this index, the agoraphobic or other interested parties can quickly turn to specific pages and get more understanding and answers to individual problems.

Foreword

Living is a challenging process. Living well is even more so. We need all the help we can get. From the moment we are born, we have experiences that impact upon us and we carry these experiences with us throughout our lives. We are the sum total of our heredity, our environment, and our life experiences. We would be severely limited, and life would be extremely difficult, if all we knew came only from our own experiences. Fortunately, we learn a lot from one another. We are students and teachers. Our very survival is dependent upon how well we learn, and apply what we learn. Learning and application is very much related to the skill of our teachers.

Melvin Green has been a student of agoraphobia. He knows it well. He has experienced it first hand, has lived with it, has researched it, and has learned its ramifications. Fortunately for us, he is also a skilled teacher and has given us an opportunity to learn from his experience. In order to maintain hope and motivation to go on, it is essential that we profit from the pain, the fear, the anxiety, the depression, and all the upsetting emotions that life brings to us. In his journey, Mel has clearly experienced it all, has been able to identify it, understand it, resolve it for himself and communicate it in this book so that we can learn from his experience.

Agoraphobia has elements that are a part of every human being's existence. To some extent, we all will recognize parts of ourselves in these pages. Hopefully, we will use that recognition to further our understanding of ourselves and others, and explore our alternatives. Through the use of personal examples, case histories and letters, we are given illustrations that make it clear that agoraphobia is not just a theoretical problem, but a real life issue for millions. The journey that Mel has been on has had many twists, turns and detours, and it would be easy for anyone on such a trip to get lost. Mel did not get lost and did not lose his drive. He has done his homework exceedingly well, and he has drawn an exceptionally detailed road map showing the way out that can help others that follow to also find the way.

Lee M. Shulman, PhD.
Beverly Hills, California
May, 1985

Preface

AGORAPHOBIA, the most common and disabling of all phobias, may afflict as many as 22 million Americans.

Sufferers of agoraphobia are subject to attacks of sudden panic that can strike at any time, for no apparent reason.

Many agoraphobics cannot go shopping, drive a car or eat in restaurants. Their lives are limited by the condition and just daily functioning may be greatly difficult.

Many will not venture beyond their front doors. They are prisoners in their own homes, victims suffering unknown fears which prevent them from participating in life.

"LIVING FEAR FREE" is written by a recovered agoraphobic who has many years of experience in counselling agoraphobics. He is a Founder of the New Beginning Foundation for Agoraphobia, a national organization that has helped hundreds of agoraphobics attain recovery. It is written in simple, lay language and contains common sense answers to the complex subject of agoraphobia.

"LIVING FEAR FREE" will aid those afflicted with this condition by providing a clear, concise guide to help them understand, and deal with, the problems created by agoraphobia. It will also enable those close to the agoraphobic, family and friends, doctors and therapists, to better understand and be of greater benefit in helping the agoraphobic attain his or her recovery.

"LIVING FEAR FREE" provides the answers to understand the causes and deal with the physical symptoms and feelings of agoraphobia, techniques in controlling stress and anxiety, prevention of the feared panic attack, and necessary changes to attain recovery. Case histories will help the agoraphobic relate to his or her condition and realize that she is not alone.

"LIVING FEAR FREE" was written with love and concern for the agoraphobic. It should be part of every agoraphobic's program for understanding and ultimate recovery from this debilitating condition.

Acknowledgments

I believe that all of my life experiences have led me to write this book. Part of those experiences was having contact with many people who have affected my direction and added to my personal growth.

I wish to acknowledge the following individuals and thank them for being there when I needed them:

Dr. Maurice Weiss (deceased)—For being my friend when one was so desperately needed and for starting me on my road to recovery.

Kathleen Cornell—For being there when I needed her and for giving me the support, input and encouragement to continue with this book.

Gil Boyne—For introducing me to hypnosis and tolerating me during the years I studied under him.

Dr. Claire Weekes—For making me aware that there was a direction of recovery from agoraphobia that made sense.

Dr. Lee Shulman—For his encouragement and affirmation of the words I have written.

Reneau Peurifoy—Director—Peurifoy Institute, Citrus Hts, CA. for his contributions to the format of this book.

My children, Laurie and Douglas—For loving me then and now and for surviving having an agoraphobic father during their early years.

The many agoraphobics who trusted me enough to share their feelings and "educate" me on agoraphobia.

And especially to my wife Rosemary, to whom this book is dedicated, for being there when I needed her.

Many others have affected my life one way or another, and to them, a special thanks.

Profile of an Agoraphobic

1

Mommy, mommy . . . where are you? I feel so afraid. I'm all alone. My whole body feels afraid. My heart is pounding so hard and fast. Where are you, mommy? I need you near me. I feel like I'm going to scream and get hysterical. I must be crazy. I'm going to die. I feel so weak. I can hardly breathe. Mommy, mommy . . . where are you?????

A frightened child? No . . . a 35-year-old adult male, well educated, married, with two children, a successful businessman . . . but in the shadows of his mind, a frightened child. This person is an agoraphobic. This person was me.

Agoraphobia . . . the most debilitating of all phobias. A feeling of impending doom and a fear that is with you constantly. Fear of what? You don't know. What can you do about it? You don't know. What causes it? You don't know.

But, you do know this . . . your world is one of constant stress and anxiety, confusion and frustration, fear and pain. You are afraid to leave home without some trusted person being with you. You avoid any situation or event that might make the anxiety grow. You avoid people for fear that they might see through your facade and think you are crazy. No one understands. How could they? You do not understand yourself.

Literally translated from the Greek, agoraphobia is defined as "Fear of open spaces" or "Fear of the marketplace." Actually, it is neither. It is the fear of the anxiety that might lead to the dreaded panic attack . . . the panic attack that will either drive you totally insane or wrack your body so painfully that you will die.

For most of my life I was an agoraphobic, eight years of which I was severely limited. I know that my story is the story of millions of sufferers of this debilitating condition. I am telling it now so that those who read this will know that they are not alone and that others have walked down their path. I have spoken to hundreds of agoraphobics in the past years, and their story could be mine . . . and mine theirs.

Born in Brooklyn, New York, in 1932 to immigrant parents, I was the youngest of three sons. The traditional European roles of parenting were followed in my family, and my father, a plumber, worked twelve-hour days to support his family, while Mom was in charge of raising the children.

She was a fearful and frightened woman who clung to her immediate neighborhood for all her necessities. Mom never went to a movie, or restaurant, or shopped outside of the neighborhood alone. She felt most secure when she was at home. Our neighbors and friends knew you could always count on her if you needed food or needed someone to tell your troubles to, but, to her three sons, she was unable to display any signs of warmth or affection. Instead, anger, verbal abuse, and criticism were used to control the children.

I wanted my mother's love . . . a love she did not know how to show. I grew up a frightened, insecure child, always rejected, and feeling totally inadequate. In my early childhood, I can recall memories of fear and panic when Mom was not close by. I needed her love and support . . . and could not get it.

It was during my research of agoraphobia that I realized my mother was an agoraphobic. It all came together, and I now understand and forgive her. My poor mother did the best she could.

I was a fair student but did not participate in most school activities, such as athletics, because of my insecurities and fears of rejection. I was known as a "loner." I was the "good boy," obedient and compliant.

I wanted very much to be liked and strived for any affirmations I could get. In fact, at home I assumed the role of the daughter that my mother wanted and never had. I helped her clean the house. I ran her errands. I did everything I knew how to get her to say that she loved me, or that I did well. It never happened. I brought home projects from school for Mom's approval. They were looked on without comment. I had given up on Dad. We could not communicate on any level. His involvement was to earn the money, and Mom would take care of the rest.

During my high school and college years, I became better adjusted socially. I had formed a group of friends and became more involved in school activities, usually noncompetitive. They were happy years, because I received the support I needed outside of my home. However, when I met a girl who showed some interest in me, I became obsessive. I wanted her love and affection desperately. I was overwhelming. Inevitably, I was rejected. Of course, at the time I was not aware that the love I needed from Mom I was seeking from others.

I learned very early in life to develop techniques to get people to like me. I became everybody's friend. I would go out of my way to do things for them. I was liked by many and loved by none (or so I felt). Any form of rejection devastated me. During this period of my life I was not consciously aware of my inner feelings of inadequacy and insecurity. I was handling my life as well as I could, with some success. And so, I continued through college, making people laugh, seeking out relationships (and being rejected), being "Mr. Nice Guy" (you could always depend on Mel), and then I met the girl who was to be my wife. She accepted me as I was, and to this day I am eternally grateful. We dated for two years and married. Soon after, I was drafted into the U.S. Army.

While in the service, I again used all my abilities to get my superiors to like me. It worked. I became Company Clerk. I asked my new wife to leave home and join me at the army base. It was a good life. Because of the structure of service life, I was never alone (even then I was uncomfortable when left by myself). However, there were signs that I was "different." Whenever a situation became threatening to me, such as guard duty and field work, I manipulated my way out of it. It was not the assignment, but the fear of being alone. But I functioned well, and the two years were uneventful.

Upon discharge, we returned to New York, and I began working at an office. Soon after we settled into civilian life, the feelings that I had stifled for so many years started to come to the surface. I was starting to experience a low grade of anxiety and uneasiness. Things just did not feel right. I was always feeling "uncomfortable." I could not explain the sensation. I went to my family doctor, and he said it was nerves. He prescribed a tranquilizer. It helped for a while and then did not seem to do the job. So I increased the dosage.

Before long, I was taking eight pills a day. Still, the strange feelings were there. I started making adjustments to my discomfort. I drove to work instead of taking the subway. At work, I spent a lot of time in the restroom trying to compose myself. I was very confused . . . and scared. I did not know what was happening to me.

And then it happened . . . my first panic attack. I was driving to work one morning and, for no apparent reason and without any warning, I started to feel dizzy. My body shook, and my heart was pounding in my chest. I couldn't breathe. I felt a fear like none I had ever felt before. I thought I was going to die.

I turned the car around and raced home. I went to bed and could not stop shaking. The next day I went to the doctor. He could not find anything physically wrong with me. By this time, the feelings of anxiety and fear were in full control. I stayed home for a week, scared and confused.

But, I had to return to work. I "conned" a friend who lived close by into driving to work with me. Wasn't that better than taking the subway? I felt better having a traveling companion. At work, I started to get closer to certain people who I felt could be of help if I had another attack. I started to create my "support system" away from home.

I spent most of my non-working hours at home. I was becoming limited in my movements. I could not stand being alone. I was in a constantly tranquilized state. Questions kept entering my mind. Was I going crazy? Was I going to die? Fear and anxiety were my closest companions. They were with me, day and night. I could not sleep well and would wake up in cold sweats. I did not know what to do. Nothing seemed to help.

My doctor suggested that I seek psychiatric help. That started my many years of therapy and counseling. During all of those years, I continued to experience the same feelings of anxiety and fear. I found that all the insight in the world did not alleviate my feelings of impending doom.

I was never diagnosed as an agoraphobic by any of the professionals I had seen. There was no lack of frightening labels that they could burden me with: Anxiety Neurosis, Severe Depressive, etc. However, I did continue therapy. What else could I do? Since there wasn't any physical reason for my problem, and the psychiatrists were not helping me, my logical conclusion was that I must be incurably insane . . . and beyond help.

One of my overwhelming fears was that I was going to die from a heart attack. The fantasy I created regarding that fear was always on my mind. Luckily, I had a sympathetic doctor whose office was across from my home. I would see him three times a week for an electrocardiogram before I left for work. His assurance that my heart was all right allowed me to function for a few days. Then the fantasy started again, and I was back in his office.

My adjustments to the condition became more and more part of my life. I became limited in my movements and did very little alone. The fear of the panic attack striking again was always with me. The anxious feelings were constant. I was confused and frightened. Different tranquilizers, mood elevators, and anti-depressants were prescribed. Nothing helped. Any joy in my life was overshadowed by the fear and anxiety.

I became morose and withdrawn. I was popping pills like they were candy in order to continue going to work. I would have preferred staying home, where I felt safe, but I had to support my family, and so I persevered. I was totally dependent on other people in order to function on any level.

I was always worried about my driving companion not being available so that I could go to work. What if he became ill? What if he had to work late and could not drive home with me? What if he went on vacation? The "what-ifs" dominated my life.

I could not discuss what I was going through with anyone but my wife and the psychiatrist. How could I describe feelings that did not have a basis in fact? For all intents and purposes, my life should have been a happy one. I had a loving wife, a lovely child, and a job. What was there to fear? Why my wife stayed with me during those years is still a mystery to me. I have asked her many times since I recovered, and the answer has always been, "Because I loved you." How she could have loved a tormented person such as I was is the mystery of the ages.

Suicide entered my mind many times during this period. It seemed like the only sensible solution. I did not feel that I was good for myself or anyone else. The world would be better off without me. But something inside of me

4

was still burning. Was it hope? I don't know. I just kept walking down the road with anxiety, fear, and depression as my traveling companions.

What still amazes me is that to outsiders it appeared as if I did not have a trouble in the world. I had developed a good sense of humor and made people laugh. They liked me. I was good at my job. I had the respect of my coworkers and superiors.

If there was a company function or an invitation for a drink after work, I always had a prior engagement, or (and I used this excuse a lot) I felt like I was coming down with a bug. ("You understand, don't you?" "Sure, I hope you feel better soon.") I had more excuses than I had hair on my head. I was the master of the side-step. I have learned since that we agoraphobics are the masters of disguise. I could have had a full-blown panic attack in front of someone, and they would never know. Amazing? Not really. I would do anything so that they would not know that I was crazy.

And then, somehow, a miracle happened. The anxiety seemed to reduce in its intensity. I don't know how or why it happened, but it did. I started to feel better. I began to feel human again. Although there were still some fears, they did not seem so bad. I began to feel a little freer and more confident. I felt that finally I was rid of this terrible condition, and, at last, it was behind me. Now I was ready to fulfill my dream . . . to move to California. The new surroundings and a new job were exciting. I was functional. Our second child, a son, was born. Life was good.

Then, one day driving to work, it struck again. The panic attack! This time it was worse than it ever was in the past. For days I lay in bed trembling. I told my wife I must have the flu, but I knew the truth. I was back where I was a few months earlier . . . but this time I did not have the support system I had in New York.

All of the old fears and symptoms returned. I could not be left alone and would not allow my wife to leave the house without me. I became totally dependent on her. I became a child, fearful and insecure.

I had to return to work and went back on the tranquilizers I had taken with me from New York. I was an emotional and physical wreck. I used the old standby excuse of a lingering flu to explain my condition. I started making adjustments. We moved closer to my office. I would drive to work following the same route every day. I knew every point of security along that route . . . every doctor's office, fire station, dentist's office, pay phone . . . any place that I could get help if the panic hit again.

If there was any obstruction or construction on my route, I would turn around and go home. It was inconceivable for me to go around the block. I did not know what was there and did not have points of security. Three blocks could have been a million miles. I proceeded from point to point until I got to the office. The distance was one mile—the longest mile in the world.

I felt moderately safe in the office. I hired a passive assistant and, unbeknownst to him, he became my support person at work. If I ever had to leave my office for business reasons, he was always at my side. I called my wife constantly to be sure she was at home should I need her. If she had to go shopping or take the baby for a walk, she called me to let me know she was going and when she would return. Those periods when she was not available for my calls were pure hell. Except for my drive to and from work, I was never alone.

One day, while going to work, I was rear-ended. I suffered a whiplash and had to go to the doctor. Little did I know that was the luckiest day of my life. The doctor who was recommended to me was to be my salvation. His name was Maurice Weiss.

I had to see him weekly for treatment. Naturally, my wife accompanied me when I went to his office. During these visits we developed a friendship . . . one that lasted for many years. I told him about my condition, and he seemed sympathetic. He prescribed tranquilizers, but . . . more importantly . . . he let me talk freely. He was non-judgemental and, even after I told him my feelings, he still seemed to like me. Of course, I transferred my dependency to him. What is better than a doctor if you have the "impending heart attack?" It was during my "I'm having a heart attack and am going to die" examinations by Dr. Weiss that he looked down at me, plugged into the electrocardiogram, and asked me a question which was to change my life. He asked, "Mel, would you rather live like this . . . or die?"

The question shocked me. I had never heard what I secretly thought of as the only solution, verbalized by someone else. And that someone else was Dr. Weiss, a man I loved as much as my own father. I was overwhelmed. The question kept running through my mind. At night, I would lay awake sweating and asking myself, "Would I rather live this way . . . or die?" I was so frightened that I disassembled a gun I had at home. I got rid of all the pills with the exception of those I really needed.

And then . . . in the middle of the night . . . came the decision. I would rather die than live this way. A feeling of calm came over me. If death was preferable, then why not tempt it? Why not start taking risks? I began by taking another route to work. I cannot tell you how anxious and fearful I was, but, I thought, the most that could happen was that I would die, and that was preferable. Sometimes the fear was overwhelming, but I kept pushing. It became a game. What was going to happen first . . . killing myself or someone else in an accident?

However, a strange phenomenon took place. As I started to accomplish more goals, I started to feel more confident. As I felt more confident, the fear and anxiety reduced. More importantly, my attitudes about myself started to change. I became more positive and optimistic. The time period it took to become fully functional was many months . . . months filled with anxiety and fear. I do not know if I would have the courage today to do it over again.

I had the full support of my wife and Dr. Weiss, and I cannot tell you how much that helped me in overcoming my agoraphobia. I will share this . . . it was the most painful period of my life. I think if I had to do it over again, the way I did, I wouldn't have disassembled that gun.

That was 15 years ago. I like to refer to that time as my "previous life-time." Since then, I have traveled extensively alone, was a top management executive in various corporations, and have been successful in business and personally.

In 1977 I decided to leave the corporate life and venture out on my own. I wasn't sure what I wanted to do, but I did know this much . . . I was happiest when I was of service to others. I thought of ways that I could make a living and still fulfill my goal of being of service. I knew I wanted to work with people, to help them, but I did not have a professional degree and felt I was too old to return to school. Then, through a fluke, (the best things in my life came to me through flukes), I took a course in hypnosis. I became fascinated with the modality. Could this be the key to help me fulfill my needs?

I learned my craft and attained my certification as a hypnotherapist. I continued taking courses and attending lectures on human behavior at local universities. I loved what I was learning, and it felt very natural to me.

I secured a position at a local mental health clinic as a staff hypnother-apist. It was there that I had the opportunity to work with my first agora-phobic. My success in helping him overcome his agoraphobia made me realize that all my life's experiences had led me to this time and place. I knew then why I had suffered the pains and frustrations of agoraphobia. I was meant to dedicate my life to helping others attain recovery from agoraphobia as I had. Who knew better than one who had been there? I thank God that I was an agoraphobic for, finally, after so many years, I AM FULFILLED!!!

What Is Agoraphobia? 2

As Founding Director of the New Beginning Foundation in North Hollywood, California, I am in contact with many agoraphobics throughout the world. The Foundation was organized to assist agoraphobics in attaining their recovery, educate the public about agoraphobia, and disseminate information to the professional community.

I receive many letters daily, and I would like to share one that is typical of the frustration created by the ongoing search for answers.

CASE HISTORY—ELAINE

Dear Mr. Green:

I found out about your organization through "Dear Abby" and hope with every hope I got that you can help me.

My only knowledge of what is wrong with me is through some literature I have found and seeing people with similar problems on TV.

I am 26 years old and married. Our income is tightly budgeted and I have been seeking answers to my problem for a long time. I cannot afford to go to any more doctors. It seems that they cannot help me. My husband listens but I'm sure he doesn't understand. I don't know if I understand myself. Sometimes I almost wish it would happen to him just once so he could see what I am going through. I love him very much but I can't be the wife I want to because of this sick thing I'm carrying around with me.

My life is very limited. I can't go to a lot of places in my own neighborhood where I've lived all my life. I can't even go for a job. It happens every time. I'm losing all my friends. I'm afraid one day I won't be able to leave my home.

I don't know what I have or what causes this. I feel like I'm having a heart attack. My heart starts beating so fast. My whole body turns into a sweaty bundle of nerves and my legs turn to rubber. It's getting so bad, I can hardly go visit my relatives, let alone sit down and have a weekend dinner with them.

The doctors gave me pills and they did not help. I saw a psychiatrist and he said it was nerves or hyperactiveness. He gave me nerve pills and they seemed to make me worse. Then he told me it was boredom and to go get a job. Just to be away from home for 5 or 10 minutes is a battle. His assistant told me that I sounded like I was suicidal. That scared me a lot.

I find myself overly depressed most of the time and I know it's because of this. I want to do so many things but having experienced this fear so many times . . . I just can't. I've told myself "you are not going to let this happen." But it always does. And I just don't know why. I just haven't any control over it. It can happen anywhere at any time. I feel like running away. But in many situations I can't so I stay and make a complete fool of myself. There is no way of hiding it. If I could I would. Feeling this way is one thing, but to have people see you like this is another.

Because of this I feel nervous all the time now. I haven't had a good nights sleep in so long, no doubt because it is working on my mind. I want so much to be normal. I know this is far from normal.

I've read this over and it sounds so stupid and crazy. But I am going to send this out because I know I need help. I hope I'm not beyond help. Am I agoraphobic or am I crazy? I'm so ashamed of it. I can't talk to anyone about it besides my husband and he looks at me like I'm crazy. Maybe I am. Please help me.

Elaine _____

Could you have written this letter? I know that when I was severely agoraphobic I could have. I have received many letters just like this, sharing years of frustration, the belief that they must be crazy, the pills, the dollars spent without results, the constant attitude of family and friends that "You can do it if you wanted to." I imagine that at one time there was a caveman who could not leave his cave because of "strange" feelings.

As recently as thirty years ago, agoraphobia was treated by a surgical procedure called frontal lobotomy, an operation in which the nerve fibers in the brain were severed to relieve some mental disorders and tensions. Thousands of agoraphobics were turned into walking vegetables by this simple surgical procedure. It was acclaimed by the medical world as the solution for the suffering. If you could not feel, you would not suffer (and also would not be a burden to society and those around you). Read or see the movies of the story of "Frances Farmer" or "One Flew Over the Cuckoo's Nest." Both used lobotomies as their theme. Then came shock treatments. This was the next step in "relieving suffering." Then, of course, the ultimate answer—"the magic pill." Hallelujah! No more surgery, no more shock treatments. Just take the little pill, and all will be well. Rejoice!!! All of this and we still have the problem of agoraphobia.

The Definition of Agoraphobia

After all these years, millions of Americans are still asking themselves the same question, "What is wrong with me?", and getting the same "non-informed" answers. It amazes me—with the thousands of words that have been written on the subject and with the exposure on television and radio of "experts" in the field—that the definition of agoraphobia still eludes them. Of course, you can always look up the word in your dictionary or in some psychological manual:

Webster's Dictionary: ag-o-ra-pho-bia (n) abnormal fear of being in open spaces.

That was not me. I was not afraid of open spaces (whatever that means). I feared a lot of things . . . but not "open spaces". . . I don't relate to this definition.

At the New Beginning Foundation we have instituted a statistical survey of those who have participated in our various programs. One of the questions on the survey is: "How did you become aware that you were an agoraphobic?" A vast majority answered in this manner: "Through seeing programs on TV about recovered agoraphobics and saying to myself, that is me."

It seems that the old saying, "It takes one to know one," really applies to us. We can go round and round, but the bottom line is that we can relate to another like us who has suffered the pains of agoraphobia, and when that happens—Eureka!—"There is a name to this condition. I'm not the only one."

And that is just the way many of us find out that we are agoraphobics. But that may only be the start of the problem. We read everything we can get on the subject, and what do we end up with? FEAR OF OPEN SPACES . . . FEAR OF THE MARKETPLACE, or some other definition that just doesn't seem to fit or feel right.

We go to our doctor, psychiatrist, psychologist, or other guru and meekly say, "I think I'm suffering from agoraphobia." The answers: "You can't be agoraphobic—you can leave your home". . . or . . . "Here's a pill that will take care of that problem". . . or . . . "Tell me about your mother" or "There is no such thing as agoraphobia". . . or . . . "All you have to do is force yourself to do it, and you can". . . or . . . or . . . or . . . you can add your own experiences to this scenario.

Please understand, I am not condemning the medical or psychiatric professions. They are doing all they can to help. The problem is in the diagnosis and misunderstanding of agoraphobia. When the patient comes in with vague fears and anxieties, the doctor will treat it as he has been trained to do. For most people, medication is an answer. But, unfortunately, not the agoraphobic. Although the medication might subdue some of the feelings of anxiety, it will not eliminate the feelings of fear that create the anxiety.

I now submit a definition of agoraphobia that I know will make more sense to you. It might not make sense to those who have not suffered from this condition, but it will put you on the right road to seeking proper help.

Mel Green's Dictionary: ag-o-ra-pho-bia (n) *Fear of the anxiety that can lead to panic.*

THAT'S IT! Isn't it simple? If we did not get those "strange" feelings when facing a situation or event, would we have any problems? Ask yourself this question: "Am I really afraid of the place or situation I am in . . . OR . . . am I afraid of the feelings I might have . . . feelings of fear, stress, anxiety, and eventually PANIC? You are not fearful of supermarkets, automobiles, restaurants, shopping malls, or anything out there. You are afraid that you might experience a panic attack away from your "safe place," and . . . then what??? If some wise person could eliminate the word "agoraphobia" from the English language and replace it with "anxietyphobia" or "panicphobia" perhaps we could get more understanding and help. It makes sense, doesn't it?

The "civilians," as I like to call those who have not suffered or experienced agoraphobia, totally misunderstand what agoraphobic panic is like. What I tell them is, "If you have ever experienced what you consider panic in your life, multiply those feelings by 20 or 30. You might then be *close* to what agoraphobics feel when they experience panic." How often I have heard this statement from the "civilians": "Well, I am sometimes anxious and nervous and sometimes even feel panic, but I don't act the way she does." I tell them to thank God that they don't.

We, who have experienced agoraphobic panic, know two things when it happens: (1) We are going to die, and (2) We must be going crazy. The symptoms you are having are "perfectly normal." We will get into this in future chapters.

Over the years, I have given many lectures on agoraphobia and have been on television, and radio discussing the subject. I will go anywhere at any time to educate the public and help create more understanding of this condition. When given the opportunity, I like to create the following scenario for the interviewer and audience. It sometimes seems to give them a better understanding of what we are dealing with.

"Mr. Interviewer, if you can, imagine that you are leaving your house this morning on your way to the studio. All seems well, but as you are walking down the path, suddenly, from out of nowhere, appears the biggest man you ever saw. He has a baseball bat and, for no reason, hits you on the head. You stagger back into the house, not believing what just happened. When you are feeling better, you peek out the door, and everything seems normal. You start down the path again. Suddenly, he is there, and again you are struck. You get back into the house where you are safe. You look out the back door . . . he

12

is there. You look out the windows . . . he is there. You know if you leave the safety of your home, you will be hit again. QUESTION: Would you leave?"

When I was interviewed by Michael Jackson, the syndicated radio personality, his answer was, "Heck, no. I would broadcast from my living room. There is no way I would leave the house." Of course he wouldn't. No sensible person would. No one in his right mind would subject himself to pain. Now, and here is the reason for the scenario, if you could relate to the baseball bat as being the feelings of extreme fear—fear that creates pain and panic—you might be able to understand why agoraphobics will not venture forth without some "protection" (the support person), or perhaps will not venture forth at all. We are doing the most normal thing in the world—we are protecting ourselves. We do not want to be "hit on the head," although many of us feel that would be preferable to the feelings we have.

Most agoraphobics would be happy to change places with anyone who is dealing with a physical illness, even cancer. At least they would be understood and could be treated for their illness. When you are physically ill, everyone rallies around. "What do you need? . . . How can I help? . . . Oh, you poor thing . . . If you need me, call." When you are dealing with anxiety . . . fear . . . panic, where is everyone? No one is there to rescue. "What is there to be anxious about? . . . There's nothing to fear . . . Grow up." There is quite a difference. Thank God, there are those who have some understanding and want to help. God bless them. But as a rule, we agoraphobics are the illegitimate children of the world, misunderstood and, at best, perhaps tolerated.

The Agoraphobic Panic Cycle

I know that agoraphobia can be a very complex subject. I have held 30-hour training seminars for professionals and have spent 20 of the 30 hours in explaining the agoraphobic personality and "What is Agoraphobia." And yet, in the complexity is a simplicity.

There is a "cycle" involved that must be stopped in order for the agoraphobic to attain calm control once again. The cycle is started when something causes them to think a fearful or anxious thought subconsciously which produces tension. This triggers the sympathetic division of the autonomic nervous systems. This is the part of our nervous system that causes involuntary actions. The thought creates unpleasant feelings and symptoms. The increased unpleasant feelings cause more fear, *ad infinitum*. We are soon in a full blown panic attack. The key in preventing the panic attack is to break the cycle.

This can be done in various ways. At the New Beginning Foundation, we teach the agoraphobic how to control the stress and anxiety with the use of audio cassettes that utilize a self hypnosis process. These tapes differ from others in that the "programming" involved includes a very powerful post-hypnotic suggestion that the agoraphobic can use at any time to reduce the levels

13

of anxiety immediately. Other relaxation cassettes can be useful, but it is the posthypnotic suggestion that cause the stress and anxiety to reduce upon command.

In future chapters, I will discuss other techniques to control the stress and anxiety in more detail.

A Physicians Guide to Diagnose Agoraphobia*

As I have indicated earlier in this chapter, there can be difficulty in the diagnosis of agoraphobia based on the vague symptoms supplied by the patient. I am, therefore, submitting a simple screening method for physicians to determine whether a patient may be suffering from agoraphobia. This screening procedure is designed for physicians and other mental health professionals to provide them with a quick and easy way to decide if a patient has a high probability of having agoraphobia. It is aimed primarily at what the *Diagnostic and Statistical Manual of Mental Disorders (Third Edition)* classifies as "agoraphobia with panic attacks" (300.21), since that is not only the most common form of agoraphobia, due to the symptoms usually associated with agoraphobia, but also the kind the physician is most likely to encounter.

A physician should be alerted to the possibility that a patient has agoraphobia whenever any one or a combination of the symptoms listed below is present and,

(A) The symptoms are occurring in circumstances other than during marked physical exertion or in a life-threatening situation, usually during periods of apprehension or fear and,

(B) No organic cause for the symptoms has been found leading the physician to suspect a mental or emotional cause.

Possible Symptoms Indicating Agoraphobia

1. Dyspnea (difficult or labored breathing)
2. Palpitations
3. Chest pain or discomfort
4. Choking or smothering sensations
5. Dizziness, vertigo, or unsteady feelings
6. Parasthesias (tingling in hands, feet, or head)
7. Feelings of unreality or disorientation (depersonalization or derealization)
8. Hot and cold flashes
9. Sweating

*"Overcoming Agoraphobia", Peurifoy Institute

14

How Tension Causes Unpleasant Symptoms and the Development of a Vicious Cycle

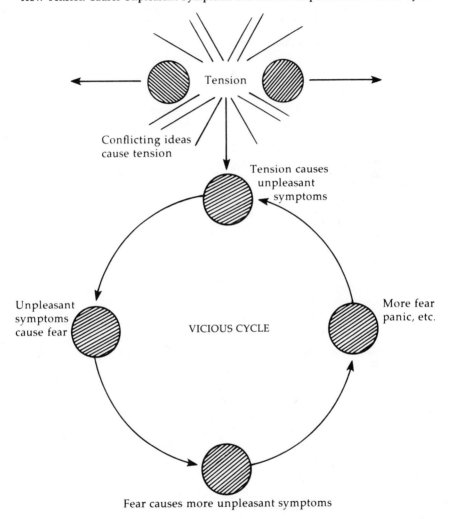

Tension

Conflicting ideas
cause tension

Tension causes
unpleasant
symptoms

Unpleasant
symptoms
cause fear

VICIOUS CYCLE

More fear
panic, etc.

Fear causes more unpleasant symptoms

10. Faintness

11. Trembling or shaking

12. Fear of dying, going crazy, "making a fool" of oneself, or doing something uncontrolled during an anxiety or panic attack.

13. A feeling of "impending doom"

Criteria Used to Confirm Need for Referral

After a thorough physical examination, a few minutes of conversation should be sufficient to determine whether or not the patient has met the following criteria. If *all three* criteria are met, then the possibility of agoraphobia should be considered. In such cases, referral should be made to a professional specifically trained to counsel agoraphobics and to determine whether or not the patient is truly agoraphobic and to provide proper counseling.

A. The patient has experienced severe anxiety and/or panic attacks

The fear and/or anxiety experienced ranges greatly from person to person and situation to situation. In its extreme, it causes the agoraphobic to flee from the situation or event that they are in and seek a person or place that they consider "safe." In its milder forms the agoraphobic can function fairly normally, but experiences mental and/or emotional discomfort with low grade anxiety being present. The fear and/or anxiety is frequently accompanied by the symptoms listed.

B. There is no apparent external cause, no basis in reality, for the anxiety and/or panic attacks

The anxiety and/or panic attacks can occur at any time and at any place . . . at a store . . . in bed, while driving or walking etc. The key element to look for is the absence of a reasonable external threat that could have caused the anxiety and/or fear.

C. The patient limits themselves in some way

Limitations usually involve the avoidance of situations or events that are associated with the anxiety and/or panic attacks. There is also frequently the need for the presence of a friend or other trusted person (the "support person") to ensure that help is available in case of sudden incapacitation and that escape is possible from places where escape might otherwise be difficult during a period of fear and/or anxiety.

The specific limitations that an agoraphobic places on himself vary greatly from person to person. Also, while limitations may be minimal at the onset of agoraphobia and may wax and wane during its course, there is usually increasing constriction of normal activities until fear and/or avoidance behavior dominates the individual's life.

To all of you who have suffered or are suffering from this condition, educate your physician or therapist. You could be saving someone else from experiencing the pain and frustrations you have experienced. The world must be made aware that agoraphobics are not "crazy people," and that proper diagnosis and treatment are available.

Understanding Your Condition

3

"What is happening to me? Why can't the doctors find out what is wrong? It must be serious or I wouldn't be having these symptoms. The chest pains must be a heart condition . . . the headaches and dizziness must be a brain tumor . . . the shortness of breath must be lung cancer. Why can't they find out what is wrong? I read about hypoglycemia . . . maybe that's it. But the tests were negative. Maybe vitamins are the answer. There's something wrong . . . I know it. I'll go to another doctor. Surely he will find a reason for these feelings I am having. I'm taking my tranquilizers, but I still feel scared. What if I become an addict? I read somewhere that there is a chemical imbalance that causes panic. They say that there are new pills but I'm afraid of pills. What if they make me feel worse? What if I really go crazy? They will put me away. I'll spend the rest of my life in an insane asylum. What is wrong with me? There must be an answer. Why can't the doctors find the reason?????"

An agoraphobic repeats this mental exercise because he or she cannot conceive that the suffering from the continuing symptoms and feelings is not being caused by some disease or physical condition . . . perhaps one so rare that all of the medical tests and all of the doctors cannot find the cause.

The frustration and confusion is overwhelming for the agoraphobic. The cycle they follow is trying to find an answer is as follows: (1) It must be physical (2) Go to the medical doctor (3) Have physical examination and tests (4) Tests are negative (5) Doctor prescribes tranquilizer (6) Tranquilizers help some, but they still feel fear (7) Lifestyle starts to become limited because of fear and anxiety (8) Return to medical doctor who may try new drug or refer to a mental health professional (9) Period of psychological therapy, but "they don't understand" (10) Life becomes more limited, feelings of anxiety become more frequent (11) Feelings of confusion, frustration and hopelessness (12) Still feels that symptoms have a physical cause (13) Start again at #1.

This cycle is typical of how, at the onset, an agoraphobic deals with the problem. It is the denial that the cause is not physical and the frustration of not having the cause diagnosed that creates the overwhelming concern of insanity or some elusive disease.

"It Must Have a Physical Cause"

We have learned from our earlier experiences in life that there are *logical* reasons for feeling fearful or anxious. A large dog snarling at you will create feelings of distress, but you can point to the dog as the reason for the anxiety and fear. However, in the case of the agoraphobic the feelings are there, but not the dog. Agoraphobics cannot identify the cause of the feelings, and therefore conclude that it is something "out there" creating the anxious and fearful response but they do not know what it is. Since they cannot identify the cause for the feelings, the logical conclusion is that it must be physical. This decision also enables us to avoid facing the possibility that the feelings might have a mental or emotional cause, which would confirm our greatest fear . . . that we must be crazy. Also, those around us, our family and friends, reinforce our belief in a physical cause by encouraging us to seek more and more medical opinions.

I know that many of the readers can identify with all that preceded this paragraph. In my counseling agoraphobics over the past five years, I have heard this chain of events hundreds of times. As a matter of fact, I followed the same road when I became actively agoraphobic. In all of the years I was in therapy and analysis, not once did I hear the word "agoraphobia." I have had many labels for my problem and used many drugs, but the end result was I still had the anxiety and fear. I was also sure it was physical and spent thousands of dollars investigating any possible source of help. After many disappointments, I realized that I had to overcome this on my own. Be thankful that more and more of the professional community are becoming aware of this debilitating condition and that help and understanding are available.

As I have indicated, I have counseled hundreds of agoraphobics and over a period of time, certain beliefs that I had were confirmed. The cause of agoraphobia is not a mental disorder in the true meaning of the word, but a series of *learned responses*. Yes . . . you have *learned* to be agoraphobic by the same subconscious internal process that you have learned all your emotions.

Childhood Programming

The agoraphobia you are suffering from today can be traced to your early childhood. Although there may be exceptions, in most cases the adult agoraphobic had parents who were agoraphobic themselves, or, were super critical, or, stifled the child's emotions, or, were extremely fearful, or on the opposite side of the scale, over-permissive. It could be all or some of the above. The child who accepts this negative input from the parents as a reality has a particular sensitivity. Whether this sensitivity is genetic or not is unknown. An agoraphobic parent does not necessarily have an agoraphobic child. However I know this sensitivity exists. There will be more about this later in this book.

Given this negative atmosphere, the child develops a subconscious emotional belief system of feeling fearful, insecure and inadequate. The child does not receive the nurturing, love and understanding needed and very early in life comes to the emotional, subconscious conclusion that he/she does not have worth. The levels of self esteem and confidence are minimal. The child strives to get the love and understanding needed and concludes that everything she does must be perfect to attain the parents approval.

If the child comes home with a report card of straight "A"s the question is asked, "Why aren't you class president?" If the child shows emotions such as anger, the emotion is stifled. The child is not allowed to show inner feelings. If the child wants to risk, the parent instills fear of risk. If, on the other hand, the child is allowed to do anything he/she wants, the emotional belief is that the child does not have enough worth for the parents to be concerned or care.

As a child, you did not have the ability or knowledge to stand in judgement of your parents and therefore you concluded early in life that these negative messages are true and accurate.

And thus, the life script or belief system developed is . . . "Don't take risks. They will lead to catastrophic results" . . . "Little girls do not get angry" . . . "Big boys don't cry" . . . "Always strive for perfection . . . mistakes are unacceptable" . . . "The world is a fearful place" . . . "There is only right and wrong, good and bad" . . . "You always make the wrong decision. Ask me (the parent) first" . . . "Always try to satisfy my needs, but I will never let you know if you are doing so" . . . "You are incapable of functioning without my advice or help", and so on.

Can you see the pattern and relate these messages to those that you received as a child? Can you understand that the life script or belief system you developed could not be avoided? Understand, these messages were not given with malicious intent. Your parents were reacting to their own life scripts and belief systems. They did not wake up one morning and decide that they were going to make you an agoraphobic in later life. What you are reading is information for understanding, not an excuse to point a finger of blame. There is no blame, just a set of circumstances. Yes, you were dealt a bad hand . . . but, *you do not have to hold onto that hand.* You can throw in the cards and draw a new hand when you realize, as we proceed, that *you are in control of the game.*

The Development of Agoraphobia

Usually the teenage years of the agoraphobic are fairly normal. There might be some problems such a socializing or participating in school activities, but, these are minimized by the changes that take place in growing physiologically from a child to an adult. Peer pressure might force the teenager into taking risks, but he/she does not do so with comfort. There may be feelings of anxiety, but these are blamed on the "growing years." Frustrations are expected during this period and are considered normal. But, the agoraphobic teenager feels "different" in some way. The parental influence is still an integral part of his or her life. The negative input is still there, reinforcing the childhood belief system. They are usually good, obedient students. They try very hard to please their teachers and friends. And, as before, are still trying to get the love and understanding so desperately needed from their parents.

When their education is over and they are facing their adult years and the challenges of life, they are emotionally unprepared. As long as things are going well, they function well. But life has a way of playing tricks on us. Circumstances, situations or events can cause great concern. Life experiences such as marriage, birth of a child, job loss, job promotion, loss of a loved one, a serious illness, financial insecurity or other traumas can arise which result in the feeling of being overwhelmed. And, this is the turning point. The person that was a "latent agoraphobic" for all the years, now becomes an "active agoraphobic."

It is a "normal" adjustment for the subconscious mind to regress back to a childlike state and the childhood belief system when faced with the feelings of being overwhelmed.

To illustrate this, think of someone you know that may have been seriously ill, or perhaps lost a job, or experienced the death of a loved one. In order to help this person, don't you nurture them, give them love, hold them, reassure them? In fact, don't you treat them as if they were needy children? Of course you do. This is the proper response to the needs of someone who is overwhelmed by the circumstances of life. They regressed back to a childlike state. That is what happened to you when you were overwhelmed. However, think of the emotions that you had as a child and your childhood belief system. That is what you regressed back to and that is where you are today.

You are dealing in certain areas of your life as an emotionally fearful, insecure, inadequate child.

If you can think objectively of your reactions to your life today . . . the feelings of insecurity, fear and inadequacy . . . are they not the same feelings you had as a child? Ask yourself, do you not feel "childlike" in your emotional being? Now please understand, I am not saying "childish". Childish has to do with actions, childlike has to do with emotions. There is a great difference.

Aren't you still seeking the love, support and understanding of a parent (your support person) that you did as a child? Don't you feel more secure and safe when you are with someone you trust (the parent)? Isn't there a feeling of childlike dependency? Aren't you reacting to your life and the world around you in a "childlike" manner?

If you can accept this as fact, then many of the questions that you have been asking yourself can be answered. Accept that this is the cause of your agoraphobia and the solutions to the problem will be easily attainable. Accept this information as fact, and you are on the road to recovery.

The Agoraphobic Belief System

Agoraphobia is a complex subject. However, in the complexity there is a simplicity. By acknowledging that we are dealing with our world in a childlike manner and realizing why we are doing so, we can be taught to make the adjustments necessary to overcome agoraphobia once and for all.

To begin with, we must understand the workings of the subconscious mind. It is at the subconscious level that our problem exists and that the feelings that create the symptoms of agoraphobia eminates from. The subconscious mind can be compared to a computer. It is a storehouse of information containing everything you ever felt, thought or experienced. In other words, all of your life experiences, negative as well as positive are stored there. The subconscious mind does not know the difference between good and bad, right and wrong, fantasy or reality. It is non-judgemental.

Like a computer, it responds to signals and does so by sending out messages to the physical body and conscious mind. The body and conscious mind react accordingly. If the message sent is one of joy, you will react by feeling joyful. If the message is sadness, then you will feel sad. This is different than thinking a conscious thought of joy, such as listening to a funny story and laughing. What I am describing are the inner feelings of joy and all of the other feelings we call emotions. Since the subconscious "computer" contains all of your life experiences, it also has programmed into it your childhood belief system. As we have learned, it is that belief system that is creating the agoraphobia we are dealing with today.

It is important that you accept that your childhood belief system as an integral part of you. It cannot be eliminated nor is there any pill that will change what you have experienced and internalized as a child. This is not all negative, since there are parts of your childhood that are very beneficial in your adult life.

Developing a "Non-agoraphobic" Belief System

Since we know that living our lives as adults using the childhood belief system is not working for us, we have to develop an alternative belief system that will work better. This new *alternative belief system* will allow you to live your life as a normal, confident, self sufficient, independent person without the frustrations and pain of agoraphobia.

This is done by literally *reprogramming* the subconscious mind (the computer) by introducing new, positive, affirmative, confident thoughts and ideas that develop into *new attitudes* or the *alternative belief system.* By using techniques such as those used at the New Beginning Foundation, the new programming becomes part of the subconscious and the messages that are sent to the body and the conscious mind change. It is similar to reprogramming a computer. The new programming creates new messages. Instead of fear, the new message is confidence . . . instead of anxiety, the new message is calm . . . instead of I can't, the new message is I can if I want to . . . instead of being afraid to be alone, the new message is being comfortable being alone. The fact of the matter is, if the attitudes are proper and correct for you (not right or wrong) the symptoms you are having will not exist. The alternative belief system, once internalized, eliminates agoraphobia from your life forever.

I have been recovered from agoraphobia for 15 years, and not once during that period of time have I had an agoraphobic attack. Why? Because I have learned the attitudes necessary to deal with my life in a positive manner. When an old memory comes back (and they do periodically) it does not create a reaction of fear and anxiety. As a matter of fact I chuckle at my ability not to react. In my work at the New Beginning Foundation I have guided and taught hundreds of agoraphobics these new attitudes and shared in their growth and ultimate recovery. There is no greater joy than to realize that I have helped another sufferer lead a normal, functional life. I am blessed.

CASE HISTORY—SUSAN

I would like to share a case history of a lady named Susan. Susan is 35 years old. She is married and has one child, a daughter. She was raised in a home where her father was a borderline alcoholic and her mother was a passive, fearful woman. She has early memories of trying to win her father's love. She remembers doing things that she felt would please her father, but instead of praise received rejection. Her mother was fearful of contradicting her father and was a passive, non-involved woman.

She recalls being a frightened child who panicked when her father brought her to school for the first time. When she began to cry, she was told that if she didn't act like a big girl, she would be punished. The parting gesture from her father, as he turned and left her, was a slap on her face.

Eventually Susan adjusted to her environment and was a good student. She was compliant and obedient and her teachers liked her. She participated in some school activities where she felt safe and enjoyed her school years. However, when she brought home school projects and good report cards, rather than the praise she needed, she received rejection. She could not seem to do anything good enough to receive her father's approval. Any approval she did receive came from strangers such as teachers and friends. It wasn't the same as receiving it from her father.

Her mother instilled fear in Susan by not allowing her to take risks, and, sometimes she was not allowed to take part in school activities because of her mother's fears of what might happen. She was taught that she could not trust her own judgement. Before taking any action or reaching a decision, she consulted with one of her parents. She was a shy girl and did not participate in many of the school social functions. She did not go to her senior prom because she did not have a date. Her father put her down for this.

She met her husband when she was 19. He was a friend of her cousin and they were introduced on a blind date. He seemed very strong and self assured and took Susan under his wing. He helped her get out more and she felt secure when she was with him. He was very protective of her and would not allow her to try new things unless he was with her. He was supportive of her when she did the things he wanted her to do. If she rebelled or became assertive, his reaction was anger. However, Susan did feel protected and needed and they married.

She was a compliant and passive wife and did what she could to get her husband's approval. She learned not to be assertive or aggressive. For the most part, her life was peaceful and she fit into the role of housewife easily. She was most comfortable when she was with him. She rarely went out socially without him. She did not like to eat alone in restaurants and she did her shopping in local smaller stores. If she wanted to go to a large shopping mall, it was usually with him. She was content with this arrangement and her life was peaceful.

When she gave birth to her daughter she was disappointed. Her husband wanted a son and she felt that she had failed him. Her daughter was the joy of her life. She took great pleasure in taking care of the child. Her husband became resentful of the time taken away from him and his needs and he became very critical of her. He told her that she could not do anything right . . . even give him a son. Old feelings started to emerge and, as she did with her father, she tried to win her husbands approval. The more she tried the more rejection she received. He seemed to take great pleasure in putting her down. She was feeling more and more insecure. She was feeling inadequate. She was fearful of losing her husband, the only security she had. She was afraid of sharing these feelings with anyone because she felt that she did not have the right to have them. After all, he did not beat her. He worked steady and took care of her and her child's needs. Others had it worse than she did. She should be grateful. The conflicts between her feelings and justifying conscious thoughts created great confusion and she started to feel overwhelmed. She was becoming nervous and couldn't seem to do anything right.

One day while doing normal shopping in a local supermarket, she suddenly started to shake. Her body was trembling from within and she felt weak and faint. Her heart was beating rapidly and she felt that it would burst through her chest. The worst part was a feeling of fear such as she never experienced before. She felt that she was going to die. She grabbed her daughter and fled the market. She does not know to this day how she got home. When she did, she started to feel better. The symptoms subsided and she felt calmer. She told herself that she must be coming down with the flu and spent the next two days resting. When it was time for her to go shopping again, she felt mildly apprehensive. The closer she got to the supermarket, the more nervous she felt. When she walked through the door her heart was beating rapidly and her breath was labored. She went in only a few steps and the feeling of impending doom and fear hit her once again. She fled home and when she regained her composure, called her doctor.

When she arrived for her first appointment, she didn't know what to tell him. She tried to explain as best she could what happened, but she could not describe the feelings. He examined her and told her he could not find anything wrong. He said it was probably just her nerves and prescribed a mild tranquilizer. She was afraid of taking the tranquilizer and instead of the 5 mgs. three times a day that he prescribed, she took 2½ mgs. once a day. She tried to explain what had happened to her husband but he just shrugged it off as a "woman's problem."

She was developing feelings of a low grade anxiety that was with her all of the time. She started to make adjustments to her symptoms. She was very fearful of a reoccurence of the attack she had in the supermarket, so she asked her husband to do the shopping. He complained, but he did it. She became more and more fearful of doing other things, such as driving alone. She avoided people as much as possible, for fear that they could see inside of her and think she was "weird." She returned to the doctor and he suggested that she increase her dosage. She started to take 5 mg. once a day. It didn't seem to help. Although she felt less anxious, she always lived with a feeling of fear and impending doom. She became over-protective of her daughter and wanted her within her sight as much as possible. She would leave home only when she was with her husband. She was very frightened and confused. She was afraid of sharing her feelings with anyone for fear that they would think she was crazy. During the Christmas holidays, she told her husband that she was coming down with the flu and that he should take her daughter to visit her parents for Christmas dinner. She stayed home trembling and crying.

Her doctor suggested that she see a psychiatrist. She was frightened to see one, but felt that it was her only hope. She went to him for a year, without any visible changes. They tried new medications, but they did not have the desired results. He told her she had "free floating anxiety combined with severe depression." Her husband complained about the cost of therapy and she stopped seeing the psychiatrist. She felt very alone.

One night she was watching television and turned on the Health Cable. I was being interviewed by Regis Philbin and I was describing the agoraphobic. She could not believe what she was hearing. I was describing her. She took out her dictionary and looked up "agoraphobia." It read "abnormal fear of being in open spaces." That could be her. She woke her husband and told him what she had just seen. He said "That's nice" and went back to sleep. The next day she called her doctor and told him of what she had learned. He told her that he was not familiar with agoraphobia and she should return to therapy. She knew that this was not a solution since her husband would not pay for further extended therapy. She felt that she had to talk to the person she saw on television and called the television station. They told her the program was made in Los Angeles. After much seeking, we finally made contact.

We spent an hour on the phone. When I told her that there were millions just like her, she was stunned. She had felt she was the only one. I explained to her that she was not crazy and described the approach we take to counselling agoraphobics. We sent her our informative brochure and one week later she joined our "At Home" program.

The first step was to teach Susan techniques to control the feelings of anxiety that she was experiencing. She was responding well to the programmed cassettes and called us weekly with progress reports. When she realized that she had control of the anxiety and could prevent it from building into the panic state, she started to go out on little trips with her daughter. She was not driving, but took walks. She felt more relaxed and cheerful. When we started the attitude change portion of the "Fear Free" process, the changes became more evident.

She started shopping for small items alone. The sense of gratification she received from these shopping trips enabled her to take larger risks with the knowledge that she could handle them. She met a girlfriend for lunch one day, and called me as soon as she returned home to share her success. I was very pleased and commended her on her progress. She has her "bad days," but has learned that this is the time to be good to herself and to learn from these days. The changes within her was recognized by others and she was very pleased with the affirmation she was receiving. I spoke to her husband and explained what Susan was accomplishing. He promised his cooperation in her recovery process.

It is now six months since Susan joined us. She has not experienced a serious panic attack in that time. She has felt anxiety, but has learned the techniques to deal with it and no longer fears it. She has learned the difference between agoraphobic anxiety and normal anxiety. She has become more relaxed about her daughter. She does not feel she is recovered, but is recovering. We have assured her that we will be with her until she does feel she is recovered. She knows now that she is a person of worth and has learned how to deal with the negatives of life. The need for approval from her father and husband is not as strong and she understands that the only approval that has meaning is the approval of oneself. She is thinking of getting a parttime job while her daughter is in school. *Susan will make it* as did the hundreds that have preceded her.

Susan is not an exception. She is typical of the agoraphobics we have helped at the New Beginning Foundation throughout the years. The reprogramming and development of the alternative belief system worked for her . . . it could work for you.

You have learned to be an agoraphobic . . . you can unlearn being an agoraphobic. Stop wasting time seeking reasons or the "Why?" of agoraphobia. That information will not create your recovery. Start thinking the *"WHAT"* of agoraphobia . . . *"What am I going to do about it?"*

I recovered, thousands of others recovered . . . AND SO CAN YOU!!!!!

Understanding Body Reactions

4

The difference between an agoraphobic and a "normal" person is nothing more than a thought. "What if" is the thought that separates the agoraphobic from the "normals".

"What if" . . . the pain in my chest is a heart attack? "What if" . . . the lightheadedness and dizziness is a brain tumor? "What if" . . . the shortness of breath is lung cancer? "What if" . . . the feelings of weakness is muscular dystrophy? . . . and so on.

For the agoraphobic there is not only the thought of "what if" but a fantasy is also created to complement the thought. The scenario can follow this direction: "I am having a heart attack. I am going to die alone. No one will know where I am or even that I am dead. No one cares. They will laugh at me. I will be thought of as a fool." And so the fantasy takes on the semblance of a reality in the mind. The fear created by the pain or the tightness in the chest, combined with the mental fantasy creates more anxiety, which creates more fear, and soon, the agoraphobic is experiencing, panic. This entire cycle from the thought to the panic can happen as quickly as a wink of an eye.

Is it any wonder, then, that agoraphobics want someone they trust close by in case what they fear becomes a reality? Or, that they want to be in a "safe place" in case it really happens?

The anxiety is relieved if the trusted person is close by or if they are in familiar, safe surroundings. The counter-acting thought is, "If it happens, I have help close by" and this thought neutralizes the fear.

Referring to the previous chapter, "Understanding Your Condition," is it not true that a child who is fearful needs the same feelings of security and experiences relief when mommy or daddy are close by? In the case of "normal" persons, is it not true that they want someone close by if they are ill or incapacitated? Of course it is. The difference is in the over-reaction that takes place in the agoraphobic's mind. Again, I repeat, the only difference between the "normal" person and the agoraphobic is a thought.

I have know agoraphobics who would choose housing near hospitals in case the "what if" they fear should occur. I have know agoraphobics who spend their days in a parked car in front of a hospital while their spouses are at work. Being close to help alleviates the fear that causes the panic. In my case, when I was agoraphobic, traveling from my home to my office, a distance of one mile, could only be accomplished because of security points I had along the route. If I had to travel any further distances, even with a support person, I first became familiar with hospital locations along the route. What the non-agoraphobic does not understand is that the agoraphobic is dealing with basic survival. We do what we have to do in order to prevent the feared and dreaded panic attack.

Unfortunately, some agoraphobics are fearful of hospitals and doctors. For them it is even more difficult. They must face the "what if" and the accompanying scenario without the benefits of the counter-acting thoughts. Their fantasy is that, if taken to the hospital, they will be found to be crazy and put away for life. Or, that the disease they are sure they have will be discovered and they will suffer a painful death. These people suffer panic attacks alone. This is particularly true of the homebound agoraphobic. More about this in subsequent chapters.

Your Body Reactions

The reaction to the "what if" thought is known as a conditioned response. In other words, it is a learned behavior pattern. It is important for you to realize that every thought will cause a physical reaction. When you think of something funny, you smile or laugh. This is a physical response to a thought. The same is true if you think of something sad. Tears will come to your eyes. This is also a conditioned or physical response. *It is normal to respond physically to thoughts.* However, if the thoughts are fearful, as are those created by the imagined scenario, the physical response will be fear inducing symptoms such as tightness in the chest, shallow breathing, dizziness, etc. The body reactions combined with the emotion of fear can build to the dreaded panic attack.

In order to fully understand how the body reacts to the negative thought processes, we must have a basic understanding of our nervous system. The central nervous system consists of two major components, which are referred to as the voluntary and involuntary. The voluntary nervous system is the one that directs our body movements such as arms, head, legs, etc. We are conscious of these movements, and since we direct them, the name voluntary is appropriate.

The symptoms caused by anxiety are controlled by our nervous system called the involuntary or autonomic system. This nervous system affects our endocrine glands which govern and regulate our body's reaction to stress. The endocrine glands use the involuntary nerves to send messages to various parts of our body, including the internal organs. Unlike the voluntary nervous system, the involuntary nervous system is not under our conscious control and is responsive to our emotions. Therefore, when we become fearful (emotion), the messages sent to the various parts of our body creates sweating, racing heart, tenseness of muscles, etc. The only way to control these physical responses is to change the messages being sent.

Within the involuntary nervous system, there are two other components called the sympathetic and parasympathetic nervous systems. The sympathetic nervous system prepares us for the message "danger" creating the "fight or flight" reactions. When the message "danger" is sent to the endocrine glands by the subconscious mind, we react by having a racing heartbeat, sweating, shallow breathing and our body is ready for "attack." It is important to remember that the subconscious mind will send the messages whether the danger is real or imagined. These physical reactions are perfectly normal and emotions such as excitement or anger will cause the same physical response.

The parasympathetic nervous system will usually keep the sympathetic nervous system in control. However, when anxiety is created, the sympathetic nervous system dominates the nervous system. This causes the secretion of adrenalin to the nerve endings of the various organs involved with the symptoms. Adrenalin also enters the bloodstream which affects other parts of our body. These physical reactions, plus the emotional fear creates the feelings of "impending doom" that is so commonly experienced by the agoraphobic.

The Physical Symptoms of Anxiety

Dry mouth, heart thumps, tiredness, indigestion, churning or rumbling of the stomach, fast heartbeats, skipped heartbeats, palpitations of the heart, sharp pain or sore tenderness around the heart, sweating, needle-like tingling in the hands and/or feet, a choking or lump in the throat, tight feelings in the chest, inability to take deep breaths, hyperventilation, a crawling sensation under the skin, a tight band around the head, disorientation or unreal feelings, eyes playing strange tricks, weakness, sleeplessness, nausea, diarrhea, frequent urination and depression.

The confusion lies in the fact that any of the above can be caused by a physical illness. Any of these symptoms should be discussed with your doctor. If no physical cause is found, then we can assume the enemy is the negative messages we are receiving from our subconscious minds. When continuous low-grade anxiety becomes a part of our lives, adrenalin is always activating us and keeping us sensitized. When the flow increases, bringing the anxiety/fear cycle to higher levels, we experience extreme anxiety and panic. It is important to remember that the entire process is an internal one and is not necessarily caused by an external situation, event or thing. The thought process

How Ideas Can Affect Organs and Glands

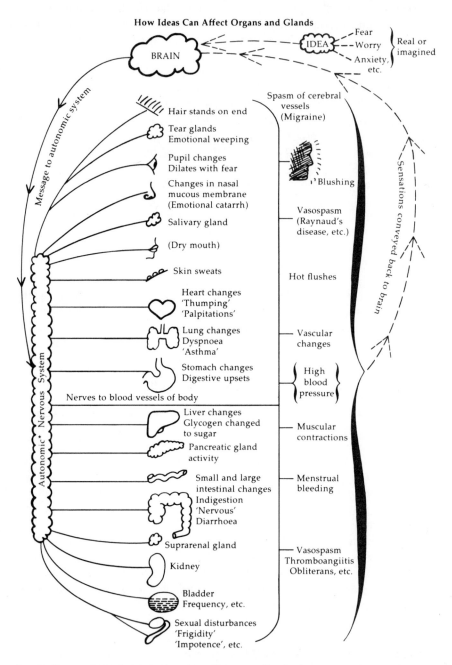

Purely diagrammatic sketch to show how ideas can affect body organs and cause changes via the autonomic nervous system.

(fantasy) alone can cause the sympathetic nervous system to react and it often does. That is why the agoraphobic can be calm one moment and anxious the next without an obvious reason. If you learn to conquer the subconscious negative thoughts, you will also conquer the anxiety produced symptoms.

By dealing with the emotions positively, you can eliminate or reduce the flow of adrenalin to the organs and muscles. By learning not to over-react to the symptoms, but instead "flow" through them by using relaxation techniques, relief will be forthcoming.

Let us explore some of the more common body reactions and/or physical symptoms and the "normal" reasons for the physical responses:

Palpitations

Palpitations are short, sudden attacks of a rapid heartbeat. They can be especially alarming and the victim usually anticipates further developments. The cause is our old enemy adrenalin, flowing in response to the message "danger" from the subconscious mind. Palpitations are usually temporary in nature and are not necessarily dangerous. By sitting calmly and "flowing through" the attack, the heart will resume its normal rate. Give yourself positive affirmations such as "this is just a flow of adrenalin. It will soon pass." and, it will.

Missed Heartbeats or "Thumping" Heart

Nervous tension, as well as stimulants such as coffee, can cause the sensation of missed heartbeats. The beats are not really missed, although they feel as if they are. They are heartbeats that are spaced irregularly and are called extrasystoles. The timing of the beat is at fault. When the heart has an unusually quick beat, it compensates by taking a restful pause so that the two unevenly spaced beats take the same time as the two even beats. The pause in between gives the feeling of the heart "stopping" or "missing" a beat. It really does not. Many normal people experience missing heartbeats, they are usually not aware of them. It is the over-reaction to the symptom that prolongs this body symptom. As with most body symptoms, use relaxation techniques to alleviate symptoms. Remember, the heart will always resume its normal rhythm when rested.

Vertigo and/or Disoriented (Unreal) Feelings

Floors seem to heave, furniture seems to sway and the body seems unsteady. These are the common symptoms of vertigo. True vertigo is not "nervous" in origin. There is usually a physical cause for this, such as, wax on the eardrum, a blocked eustachian tube or some other "real" cause to upset our equilibrium. A doctor should be consulted if you have the symptoms of vertigo. If the symptoms are disoriented or unsteady feelings, such as lightheadedness, they are probably caused by anxiety. Often, shallow breathing which causes a chemical imbalance in the bloodstream is the cause. This chemical imbalance can be compared to breathing in the exhaust fumes from your automobile. In this case, practice slow easy and deep abdominal breathing to relieve the symptoms. Just a few deep breaths can balance the imbalance. Relaxation techniques should be used which include these types of breathing exercises.

Other causes of vertigo can be low blood pressure or when normal blood pressure falls, such as in hot weather or when taking certain medications. Rising quickly from a horizontal position can create these symptoms. Women experiencing menopause often have unsteady feelings.

Inability to Take a Deep Breath

Many agoraphobics find that expanding their chests to take a deep breath difficult. This does not mean that there is anything wrong with their heart or lungs, but only that their chest muscles are tensed. Mother nature in her wisdom did not leave the act of breathing to the conscious mind. If that were so, you would not breath while sleeping. You have a respiratory center in the mind that automatically regulates your breathing. To prove this point, try to hold your breath for an extended period. You will find that in a short time you will be forced to breath against your conscious will. Usually, after this experience, you will take a very deep breath. When the tension in the chest muscles is released, the ability to take deep breaths is restored. Relaxation techniques and "flowing" are the answer to this symptom.

Hyperventilation

Hyperventilation is a very frightening experience. Not being able to breath properly creates the anxiety to fear cycle quickly. The more fearful you become, the shallower you breath, prolonging the cycle. The shallow breathing causes the intake of too much oxygen and you do not dispel the proper amount of carbon dioxide. This affects the chemical balance of the blood. Breathing slowly into a paper bag quickly alleviates the symptoms. It is necessary to break the anxiety/fear cycle so that the normal breathing can resume. Relaxation techniques are very useful. Remember, your automatic respiratory center will not allow you to stop breathing.

Tingling Sensations

The cause is similar to those in "Disoriented (Unreal) Feelings." Shallow breathing, creating the chemical imbalance in the blood, causes this symptom. Deep, slow and easy abdominal breathing will alleviate these symptoms.

Weakness

Anxiety will cause an "emotional shock" which release adrenalin. The adrenalin in the system dilates the blood vessels in various muscles, and so, the blood does not circulate adequately. When this happens, fear creates "after shocks" which continues the flow of adrenalin developing the anxiety cycle. When the anxiety (adrenalin flow) to fear (more adrenalin) to more anxiety "cycle" is broken, the weakness disappears. Constant low grade anxiety will cause the continuous feelings of weakness. Reduce the anxiety by the use of proper relaxation techniques, and the weakness will pass.

Insomnia

It is very common for anyone overwhelmed by a problem or concern to have sleepless nights. This is especially true of agoraphobics since the limitations created by the condition affects so many areas of their lives. Fears created by the "what if's", anticipating upcoming events, basic insecurities and guilts, feelings if inadequacy, all seem to rear their ugly heads at night when they are alone with their thoughts. Here are some suggestions on how to deal with those voices and messages that keep you awake.

When thoughts start inundating your mind, it is best not to fight them, but to flow with them. Assume the attitude of an objective "third party" witnessing the flow of thinking. Let your mind wander wherever it wishes, maintaining a disinterested attitude. Do not fight, but let the thoughts just flow through. Do not think about or analyze the thoughts. By doing this, you will find that the flow will lessen and that you can fall asleep.

Changing your bedtime habits and behavior can be of great help in overcoming insomnia. Sleep medications will only work for a short time, and then become ineffective. They may actually interfere with sleep. Avoid caffeine or other stimulants 3 hours before bedtime. Associate the bed with sleep, rather than eating, drinking, smoking or other activities. Watching television programs that involve you, such as the news, in bed can prevent sleep. Try not to worry about the lack of sleep. Your body will rest when it needs it.

Research the many books and articles written on the subject and find those that will work for you. Flow, don't fight, and you will sleep.

There are many other physical symptoms that the agoraphobic may suffer. I assure you that many of the symptoms are normal reactions to anxiety. Adrenalin and shallow breathing are the most common causes. Learn to relax "automatically" when the symptoms appear and they will not be as frightening or debilitating. Your body is a marvelous machine and Mother Nature has taken all of the precautions necessary to protect it. Let her do her job by not fighting but by "flowing" through these attacks. Let your body recharge itself. Practice relaxation techniques daily. Your body will respond in a positive way, replenishing the lost energy you so desperately need.

The following physical conditions can create symptoms similar to those experienced by the agoraphobic:

Hypoglycemia

Directly after eating a meal, the glucose level rises. Insulin is then secreted into the pancreas to help move sugar into the cells, and the glucose level drops. However, in people with hypoglycemia, the blood sugar falls lower than normal levels following a meal, for reasons that are not always understood. The brain, which uses glucose almost exclusively as its food, does not get enough blood sugar and sends our distress signals. The standard method of diagnosing hypoglycemia is the glucose-tolerance test. If you have been diagnosed as a hypoglycemic, as verified by your doctor, changes in eating patterns are usually prescribed as a treatment. Many doctors now believe, however, that the test results for hypoglycemia are suspect. They believe that low blood sugar levels can develop in normal people, those who do not have hypoglycemia, following the glucose tolerance tests.

The symptoms are quite often caused by "nerves" rather than hypoglycemia, and, rather than seeking treatment for low blood sugar, you would be wiser to examine the stress in your life. For most people diagnosed as hypoglycemic, relief of stress usually will remove the symptoms. Many specialists believe that hypoglycemia is a "non-disease" which is diagnosed in epidemic proportions while the number of people who have it is actually quite small.

Mitral Valve Prolapse (MVP)

Recent studies have shown that between 5% and 15% of the population might suffer from this condition. The mitral valve is a little flap valve between the left auricle and left ventricle of the heart. It is a one-way valve flapping shut when the pressure of the ventricle builds up. In MVP, one of the leaflets of the valve folds back into the auricle, where it is not supposed to be, and leaks blood in that direction. Symptoms of MVP include breathlessness, vague chest pains, palpitations, fatigue, anxiety, panic reactions, and depression. Research has shown that people with MVP have higher levels of adrenalin in their blood and are hypersensitive to the adrenalin. It is not known why this condition creates extra adrenalin secretions. MVP should be ruled out as a cause of the symptoms and can be done so by your doctor. Diagnostic equipment can be used in detecting the subtle click created by the defective mitral valve. There are various treatments available and your doctor can advise you.

Premenstrual Syndrome (PMS)

Research has shown that about 70% of menstruating women notice emotional, behavioral or physical changes in the week or so before menstruation. Symptoms can include breast tenderness and swelling, abdominal bloating, acne, craving for sweet or salty foods, irritability, depression and fatigue. Current estimates indicate that from 3% to 10% of menstruating women experience a dozen or more negative changes with such severity, that their lives are disrupted for longer periods of time. These negative changes can cause strained relationships, feelings of despair, worthlessness and loss of control.

A few years ago it was determined that PMS was caused by a deficiency of the female hormone progesterone. Because of the possible side effects of treatment with progesterone, research is now being done for alternative therapies. The consensus at this time is that PMS is created by a combination of biological and psychological causes. Most PMS researchers agree that biochemical changes are involved, but also emphasize the role of psychological, social and environmental factors. Common treatment for PMS is still the use of progesterone. However, psychological therapies and the use of other drugs to treat the symptoms directly are also being used. If PMS is your problem, your doctor should be your guide.

Relaxation Techniques

Many times in this book, I have suggested relaxation techniques as a way to relieve symptoms. There are many techniques available such as biofeedback, self affirmation, meditation and self hypnosis. In my estimation, after many years of working with agoraphobics, self hypnosis techniques are the most effective for the agoraphobic. The techniques used by the New Beginning Foundation have been designed for the agoraphobic personality and each word and sentence is well thought out for easy acceptance by the subconscious mind. The New Beginning "Fear Free" process uses self hypnotic techniques to reprogram the subconscious mind.

The agoraphobic is taught how to control the stress and anxiety by the use of special programmed audio cassettes. These cassettes differ from other relaxation tapes since they were created exclusively for the agoraphobic. They include a very powerful "post hypnotic" suggestion that reduces the levels of anxiety automatically.

There is much misunderstanding and confusion concerning hypnosis and self hypnosis. Actually, they are the same. All hypnosis is self hypnosis. The programming offered by the hypnotist, or by audio cassette, can be rejected or accepted by the recipient at any time. The media, over the years, has created a mystique of the word hypnosis and has indicated that somehow the hypnotist controls the mind. Nothing can be further from the truth. Hypnosis is simply a deep level of relaxation, which, when properly used, allows access to the subconscious mind of suggestions more directly than if this technique was not used.

With self hypnosis the user is not in a trance state but feels relaxed and calm. He is always aware of his surroundings, of sounds and movement, and can assume the normal states of awarenes at any time. If the relaxation induced by self hypnosis is elevated, the user simply falls into a restful slumber, awakening relaxed and refreshed. Contrary to rumors, there is not one documented case of a person remaining in the relaxed or hypnotic state.

Self hypnosis is a natural state of mind. Everyone experiences self hypnosis at least twice a day, once before awakening and once before falling asleep. This is commonly referred to as "twilight time." This is the time when the body and mind are most relaxed. This same "twilight time" is experienced by those using self hypnosis techniques during waking hours. Properly used, one can attain total relaxation upon command, alleviating the symptoms and feelings of anxiety. I suggest that any programming introduced to the agoraphobic be done by a certified or trained therapist that is familiar with agoraphobia so that the programming is accurate.

Biofeedback incorporates hypnotic relaxation with monitoring equipment to make you aware of the levels of relaxation and to teach you to relax upon command. It can be useful, but in my experience, agoraphobics are very uncomfortable while hooked up to the machines and this blocks the benefits. However, if you feel you would be comfortable, it is worthwhile therapy.

Another technique that I have found useful is to "shock" the nervous system to break the fear to anxiety to panic cycle. To "shock" the nervous system. a combination of minor pain and strong verbal commands are used. When you feel you are entering the cycle, slap your thigh or pinch your hand and at the same time say the word "STOP" very strongly. If you are alone, shout the word. If you are not, think the word powerfully in your mind. You can also wear a rubber band on your wrist, and snap it to inflict the pain.

A simple relaxation technique is to relax the eyelids, relaxing them so much that they simply do not want to open. This does not mean that you cannot open them. They are comfortably relaxed and you wish them to be so.

When you have relaxed the eyelids, imagine that feeling of relaxation flowing from the eyelids down your body and up the back. Once the flow has been created, imagine that your body is becoming more and more relaxed with every pass of the feelings of relaxation. While you are doing this exercise, put your thumb and first two fingers together lightly. Tell yourself that everytime you place your fingers in this configuration, you will feel as relaxed as you feel when doing this exercise.

"Flowing" through anxiety or panic is not as difficult as it seems, if proper relaxation techniques are used in dealing with life situations. Sitting calmly and allowing the anxiety feelings to peak and wane will bring relief in a short time.

Self-imagery can help in "flowing". Imagine you are at the beach watching the ocean. In the distance a small wave is forming. This represents your initial feelings of anxiety. As the wave approaches land, it grows larger and larger. This represents your feelings of anxiety growing. Soon the wave is very large and peaks. It then flows down into a smaller and smaller wave until it disperses on the beach. This image represents the start and finish of the anxiety attack. You do not fight the feelings, but "flow" with them as you flow with the image of the wave.

When the experience has passed, sit quietly for a few moments and then go on with your normal activities. Do not ponder the attack. Just accept it as you would if you had a sudden headache or sneezing spell. Do not over-react. It has passed and will not return.

As in any learning experience, repetition is the most important factor in programming the subconscious mind to respond "automatically" to the signals that create the relaxed state. Schedule specific times to practice relaxation techniques. In addition to the regular relaxation schedule, treat yourself to mini relaxation periods during the day such as after lunch, during work breaks, etc. There is a cumulative effect. The more they are used, the more feelings of relaxation are accepted by the mind and body. Properly used, the feelings of relaxation become the norm, rather than those of anxiety. When this happens, many of the symptoms will not continue to occur.

Your body has learned specific ways of reacting to signals and messages from the subconscious. Since these reactions were learned, they can be unlearned. Perseverance and patience can lead you on the road to recovery. Be good to yourself and always have faith that you can overcome this condition called agoraphobia.

Understanding and Accepting Your Feelings

5

Recently I received the following letter. I believe that it exemplifies the frustration and confusion that exists in the minds of many agoraphobics.

CASE HISTORY—CINDY

Dear Mr. Green:

I am writing to you with the hope that you could inform me of how to seek help for my problems.

I have been unable to work for the past six years. The traumas and pressures that I have had and am still going through are like a bad dream. I really can't believe what is happening to me and I really do not know what is preventing me from having a normal, productive life.

It makes me so mad that I cannot shake these feelings. They are unreal. It's really unbelievable that this is happening to me. I cannot seem to make anyone understand how or why I feel this way. I cannot understand it myself. How could anyone else?

It makes me feel different in so many ways. I feel anger and guilt towards myself for feeling this way. I seem to be such a burden on everyone around me. And I feel so resentful. I was once normal . . . why did it have to change? I see other people coming and going. It seems so simple. Why can't I?

I know there are people in much worse shape than I am. Some cannot walk, talk or see and may never be able to, except by God's will. I know that I am a lot luckier than they. Here I am with a good body not doing what others, with working organs and limbs, would or could do.

And yet, I complain. I'm the one who feels helpless. I'm the one who isn't grateful. All I can see is negatives. I don't have any confidence in myself. I feel that I cannot do anything on my own. And I worry, worry, worry, day after day. It seems like a long rerun. Anything that anyone says to me stays in my mind. I am searching so hard for answers that I cannot find. It's so confusing.

And then there's the depression. Wondering what I am doing and why I have to live this way. And, will it ever leave me or will I go crazy or freak out or die of a heart attack or have a breakdown. The thinking creates so many fears.

I am twenty-six years old. I had my first attack when I was twenty. It was one day in spring. As a matter of fact, it was March. I was cleaning out my car when I felt that I could not breath. My heart started pounding and I felt lightheaded and dizzy. And I felt a fear like I never felt before. I was very scared. I became frightened of leaving home. What if it happened again? I did not understand what was happening.

I went to an ear, nose and throat doctor. I was x-rayed and tested. Nothing showed up. I then went to a chiropractor. He said that a pulled muscle in my back was causing it. He helped, but then I felt the symptoms coming back. I went to another MD and told her how I felt. She told me it was boredom and to get a job. With a push from my mom, I did get a temporary job for one month. I hurt my back on the job and started to take muscle relaxers. My symptoms were getting stronger. I thought it was the pills, so I stopped taking them. I went to other doctors who said it was nerves or hyperactiveness. The medicines they prescribed didn't help much and they then said it was emotional and to see a psychiatrist.

My doctor referred one and he told me he would have the problem cleared up in no time. He put me on medication. From that point I saw his assistant who seemed to make it worse. I finally got so upset that one day I told her that I was not going to continue therapy. She said, "well, you sound suicidal" or something like that. I know that you do not even mention that word to someone who is depressed and dealing with fears. I began wondering if she thought I would, or was I really that bad and what was going to happen to me. Then she told me not to come if I didn't feel up to it and then told my mom the opposite. I didn't go back to her. I may have had the wrong doctors. They didn't seem to be understanding or aware of my real problems.

I want to get better, not worse. If it is my nerves, or if I am hyper, then why doesn't the medicine calm me? It's so confusing. I feel that there isn't any help for me. No one seems to understand. I can't travel to see doctors anymore. Five or ten minutes away from home scares me. I have all kinds of thoughts. I feel that I'll freak out. And when I sit at home, I just dwell on my problems. It seems I can't win for losing. It really does hurt. Only someone who knows or has been there can understand. God knows, it's rough trying to go somewhere with your thoughts running wild. It is not easy staying home all of the time being tormented by your thoughts and feelings.

Can you help me? Please help me.

Cindy . . .

How often I have heard the same story. There are variations, but the plot is the same. Fear, guilt, depression, confusion, frustration and that overwhelming feeling of hopelessness. And it is true, as Cindy wrote, "Only someone who knows or has been there can understand." When I receive a letter like this, or a phone call, I don't have to hear the words. I know the feelings behind them. However, I have learned over the years in which I have been helping agoraphobics that there are reasons and answers for these feelings. There are also many techniques that can help alleviate the symptoms and allow you to deal with your life in a fulfilling manner.

In the chapter titled "Understanding Your Condition," I indicated that agoraphobics are reacting in certain areas of their lives in a childlike manner. In order to understand the feelings of agoraphobia we must expand on this. There is a psychological therapy called Transactional Analysis. Much of what I am going to explain has to do with the theories espoused by this therapy. In order to get on to solutions, I will simplify the explanation of this theory.

In Transactional Analysis, we learn that there are three parts of our emotional personality. These are parent, adult and child. The parent part of our emotional makeup has to do with that part of us which is critical and judgemental. Conversely, it also has to do with that part which is benevolent and comforting. The adult part of our emotional personality is the analytical and "mature" part of us. The child is that part of us that deals mostly on an emotional level. It is the child within us that creates the feelings associated with agoraphobia. Therefore, the statement that we are reacting to life in a "childlike" manner means that the child within our emotional personality is dominating that personality.

When one part of our emotional being dominates consistently, we start to create conflicts with other parts of our emotional personalities. For instance, the person always reacting to life in the critical parent role will find the negatives in all situations. They try to be controlling of others and negate others feelings. Those who are constantly acting as adults will over analyze any situation and usually try to change things to their belief system. They also tend to focus on the negative. If part of you says "you should," the adult part of you says "you shouldn't or can't." The child controlling our basic emotions is in constant conflict with the adult and parent. These conflicts create stress and anxiety.

For instance, we can see from Cindy's letter, her feelings of confusion and guilt which are created by the fact that she knows she is physically capable of performing the necessary acts of living life. Her analytical adult has told her she can do anything she wants to do, and her child, being fearful, is saying to her, "she can't." There is a constant war going on inside of her. Intellectually she knows she can . . . emotionally she feels she cannot.

Unaware of the battle raging inside of her, she will try to deal with the problem in a logical manner. She hears from others, "you can if you want to" or "just face the fear and it will go away." The more she tries to do this, the more frustrated she feels. If instead, she acknowledged that the childlike fears were the real cause of the problem and dealt with them, she would have a better chance of reaching a possible resolution to the conflicts.

Dealing with the childlike emotional fears and feelings can be complicated if you do not understand the concept behind the reasons for the feelings. The concept is . . . *I am dealing in certain areas of my life as an emotionally fearful, insecure, inadequate child.* This child within me is dominating my emotional personality. Because it is dominating my emotional personality, the other parts of that personality are not being used as they should and they are in constant conflict with the child within me.

This conflict is creating feelings of fear, insecurity, confusion, depression, dependency, inadequacy, and general feelings of hopelessness. The conflicts also create the thought to fear to anxiety cycle which leads to my panics. In order to become a normal, functional person again, I must learn to balance my emotional personality so that the parent, adult and child are being used at the appropriate times. I will learn how to use the parent within me to nurture and benefit me. I will learn to use the adult within me to help me reach good and positive solutions to my problems. I will learn to use the child within me so that he or she will be the fun loving, joyful part of my personality.

In order to accomplish these goals, reprogramming on a subconscious level is necessary. The subconscious mind must develop attitudes that are positive, nurturing, affirmative, confident, realistic and, above all, beneficial for you. You must learn to use your subconscious minds constructively . . . not destructively. In my opinion, constant, repetitive, self hypnotic techniques as used at the New Beginning Foundation will accomplish these goals. This has been proven by the many agoraphobics that have become the normal, functional persons they want to be.

When working with agoraphobics, I prefer to deal with the "here and now" of situations and events. I believe that it is very important to help the agoraphobic function as best he or she can within his or her own limitations.

To help you further understand the feelings which are keeping you limited, I am going to outline some of the more common fears, their causes and alternative ways of dealing with them.

Panic

There are two fears involved in panic. The first is the initial thought or situation which starts the feelings of anxiety. Everyone, whether agoraphobic or not, experiences this first stage at times. However, with non-agoraphobics, when the threatening thought or situation passes, so do the anxious feelings.

In the case of the agoraphobic, she starts to think of what can happen in a negative manner. This is what is called the "what if's." This is the second stage or fear of panic. It is during this second stage that the fear starts to grow and the anxiety increases.

She enters the cycle of thought to fear to anxiety to "what if" to more fear to more anxiety, etc. If this cycle continues, then the agoraphobic will soon reach the levels of panic or extreme anxiety.

The cycle must be stopped in its early stage of development. The "nerve shocking" techniques plus the "flowing through" exercises described in previous chapters will stop this cycle. Relaxation techniques are to be used once the cycle is broken.

With practice and repetition, using these techniques will become automatic and be more effective everytime they are used.

Being Alone

If you can accept the "childlike" reactions to life as a reality, you can better understand why being alone is threatening. The insecure child needs the comfort of the parent (support person) nearby in case the feared panic attack should occur. The fear of being alone and dealing with the "what if's" creates the anxiety symptoms that affirms that you cannot be alone. As an aside, this was one of my most limiting feelings when I was agoraphobic. I remember them so well . . . the feelings of fear and desperation. As a recovered agoraphobic, I now prefer to be alone at times. I have learned the attitudes necessary to be comfortable and non-fearful when by myself.

When you are alone, you can use some of the following suggestions to relieve the anxiety and fear:

1. The telephone—Create a list of all the friends, relatives and acquaintances you can call if needed. Also create a list of doctors, ambulance services, paramedics, police and fire department. You are not isolated as long as you can pick up the phone. Just knowing that you can contact someone relieves the anxiety.

2. Television and radio—Watch programs which can involve you. Try to answer questions on quiz shows. Depressing soap operas can depress you even more, and depression can cause anxious thoughts. Interview programs and "talk radio" can be involving. Music is always therapeutic. Avoid the news programs. They are usually negative.

3. Neighbors—Even if you are not close friends with them, they are there if you need them. Keep that thought in mind.

4. Keep active—Activity that is engrossing will keep your mind off of your fears. Develop challenging hobbies. Read pleasurable books. Do your chores with the radio on. If you have the talent, sit down and write something. Catch up on correspondence. The idea is to keep your mind active so that you do not think fearful thoughts and to make the time pass quickly.

5. Get a pet—Pets can be good company. I often find myself talking to my dog, King. As far as I am concerned, he is the world's greatest listener and completely nonjudgemental. When he is with me, I never feel alone.

6. Attitude—Always stay in the present, affirming to yourself that "I am alright." "I am dealing with this situation." "I am safe." "Time is passing quickly" Take pride in how well you are handling the situation. You are acting like a "normal person." Look at yourself in the mirror occasionally and smile at yourself. You're doing great.

Being Overwhelmed

Many of the calls I receive from agoraphobics involve being overwhelmed by their life and the world around them. Interestingly, the caller does not realize that he or she is overwhelmed until questioned. Generally they say they feel that life is too much to deal with, or perhaps they have feelings of pessimism regarding their future.

Since I do so much telephone counselling, I have become sensitive to voices and can usually tell very early in the conversation that the caller is under stress. I then ask questions starting with "What's going on in your life right now?"

Usually there is a denial that anything of great significance is going on in their lives at this time. This is because of the belief that it is the big situations or events that create uneasy feelings. On the contrary, being overwhelmed is a series of little things that can build and soon the mind is cluttered with all kinds of fearful and negative thoughts. Mentally, the person gives all of these thoughts the same importance and they all become priority #1. They are all equally threatening and they all have to be taken care of immediately. It is like overloading the electrical system in your house. One bulb, one toaster, one iron, one fan, etc. builds up and soon the fuse blows.

There is an old saying . . . "You can't see the forest for the trees." When you are in the forest, it is dark and threatening. It is vast. Once you are in the forest, it seems there is no way out. You are overwhelmed!

If you can separate the forest into individual trees and concentrate on that tree alone, the forest is no longer threatening. Focus on each one separately, and you can deal with the forest.

A technique which I have found to be very effective in separating the many thoughts (the trees) which clutter our mind (the forest) is as follows:

1. Get a package of 3 × 5 blank index filing cards.

2. On each card write one thought or problem that is running through your mind. Be specific. Do not write "I am afraid." Write "I am afraid of being alone."

3. Do this with each thought running through your mind. Once the thought

is on paper, it becomes a reality. You no longer have to think about it. You can look at the card and remind yourself of that thought whenever you wish.

4. Take as much time as necessary to do this exercise. It is possible to have as many as 30 or 40 cards when you are finished.

5. When you feel you have put all the thoughts on cards, start putting the cards in priority order as follows:

   Priority #1—Those things you can deal with simply and easily, such as by making a phone call or writing a letter.

   Priority #2—Those things that might be a little more complicated or difficult to do, but are achievable.

   Priority #3—Those things you do not feel capable of dealing with at this time.

   Priority #4—Those things that are out of your control or may be dependent on others for fulfillment.

6. Act upon the thoughts and situations on the cards in priority order. Do not think of the next card (or problem) until you have taken care of the problem on the card you are working on.

7. Review the cards daily and change their order of priority as situations change.

8. If you deal with each tree in the forest individually, the forest becomes a peaceful glen and is no longer overwhelming.

You were overwhelmed when you experienced your first agoraphobic panic attack. It is a dangerous place for an agoraphobic to be. Use this technique as soon as you start feeling overwhelmed. Do not allow the feelings to go too far.

Depression

I often wonder why agoraphobics are so surprised when they are depressed. It seems to me that if I were living the life of an agoraphobic again, dealing with the fears and limitations, the non-understanding and rejection, the worry and guilt, I would certainly not be joyful.

Some depression is "normal" and should be expected when you are agoraphobic. However, it is what I call "justifiable" depression. It is not created by some deep, dark, mysterious psychological trauma. It is created by the reality of your life. You are not a manic depressive. You are depressed because you feel hopeless and are fed up with the life you are leading. You are angry at the world and yourself.

However, if you analyze your life and focus on more positive things besides agoraphobia, you probably can come up with some positive aspects that are giving you happiness instead of sad depression. Agoraphobics have a tendency to focus on the negatives. It takes hard work to focus on the positives, but it must be done to get through depression.

Next time you feel depressed and the feelings stay with you over an extended period of time, try the following:

Write the following contract on a piece of paper:

I, (write your name), am depressed by the life I am leading and the feelings I am having. However, I acknowledge that there are real reasons for these feelings and I am "justifiably" depressed, This depression is not a mental illness, but an emotional reaction to my lifestyle. I know it is temporary and I will not stifle or deny my feelings of depression. I acknowledge that, considering what is happening in my life, it is normal for me to feel this way at this time.

However, I do not like feeling this way and will set a time limit on how long I will allow myself to feel this way. I will allow these depressed feelings to remain with me until (write a time and date, no more than 72 hours from when you write this contract to yourself). At that time I will release these feelings of depression and will do all within my power to bring joy and happiness into my life no matter what the circumstances are. This contract is binding between me and myself, and is non-cancelable.

Signed (your name)   Time and date

Put the contract on the refrigerator door or bathroom mirror and look at it often during the time of being depressed. At the time you contracted to release the depression, fulfill the terms of the contract and start adding joy and happiness into your life.

Impatience

There is a prayer that goes "God, grant me patience, and grant it NOW!" We all want relief from our pains and frustrations, and we want it NOW! We all want to recover from agoraphobia, and we want to NOW! We all want understanding, and we want it NOW! If only I could make it all happen for you NOW! Nothing would give me greater joy. However, that is not the way it is. Not with agoraphobia or most other things in life. We have to travel a road which leads us to our goals.

All trips start with the first step. In this case, it is a "baby step." Only your inner self can determine how easy or difficult, how long or short, how smooth or hilly and how we handle the obstacles on the road we travel. It is only when your subconscious mind is accepting and willing to change that you will start taking longer and more positive steps. Your conscious mind cannot force the change. It can only help the subconscious by affirming the direction you are taking. Perseverance and persistence are your vehicle for traveling the road to recovery.

If I have learned anything in the years I have been counselling agoraphobics, it is that change will happen only when it is ready to happen. It cannot be forced by you or any therapist. When the change does take place, and it all comes together, you will find that agoraphobia is no longer part of your life. It is said that patience is a virtue. It is more than that. It is one of the main keys to your recovery. In Alcoholics Anonymous they advocate "One day at a time." In the case of agoraphobics, I advocate 5 minutes at a time. Deal with your here and now effectively, be patient, and your future will take care of itself.

Conflicts

I have written that the conflicts within us create anxiety. This is true. However, there is another aspect of conflict which can be beneficial. Conflicts can also create change. There is no reason to change if we are comfortable in our environment. Comfort can be the agoraphobic's worst enemy. *The inner pain of conflict is a strong motivator to deal with the agoraphobia.* You are forced to take some action, to create some movement to relieve the pain. Some action, any action, is better than no action at all.

If the conflict becomes too great, there is sometimes the fear of giving up. In my experience, this is very rare. We agoraphobics are survivors. We do not give up easily. When our back is up against the wall, we rise and fight. To recover from agoraphobia, you experience a form of rebirth. Sometimes, being born is painful. Let me assure you . . . it's worth it.

The pain which conflict creates will not kill you. Properly used, it will motivate you into action since action is the only way to deal with the conflict. The longer we hold onto the conflict, the longer it will be painful. Eventually we have to do something, and that starts movement.

Think back to the times you had conflicts that were overwhelming you. All seemed hopeless. However, somehow you resolved the conflict. Remember the relief you felt when the conflict was no longer with you? You had a success and the knowledge and satisfaction of your accomplishment. If you did not acknowledge your overcoming the conflict, you did yourself a great disservice. That was the time to pat yourself on the back.

Conflicts can be enemies or friends, depending on how you look at them and deal with them. If you use the pain and frustration as a motivator, the conflict is your friend. If you wallow in the conflict, it is your enemy. Know that the only way your are going to get relief is to deal with the feelings. There is no wrong way to overcome conflicts. Use every weapon you have. Call upon your inner courage and creativity. Take the risks that are necessary. Anything is better than living with conflicts. And . . . when the conflict is resolved . . . look at yourself in the mirror and say "I did good!"

Worry

Have you ever looked back on the things you worried about yesterday and wondered about why you put all that time and energy in the worrying process when the situation seemed to work out by itself? All of your worrying did not change a thing, except cause you sleepless nights and concern. Agoraphobics, as a rule, are great worriers. It is part of the negative personality.

The following is a technique I use to overcome worry:

1. Write the worrying problem on a piece of paper. Describe the problem as fully as possible. Include your feelings and fears about the problem.
2. List the things you can do about the problem on the left side of the sheet. List the things you cannot do about it on the right side of the sheet.
3. Put the sheet away for 48 hours.
4. After 48 hours, look at the sheet and see if the situation or your feelings have changed. Usually it has. You may then want to revise the list.
5. If I find that there is something I can do about the worrisome problem at that time, I do it.
6. If I feel that nothing has changed, I put it away for another 48 hours.

I have found that the thing I was worried about either resolved itself in that period of time, or that I am no longer worried as much about it.

I am not saying that all worry should be eliminated from our lives. Some worry is normal and justifiable. Things such as illness or financial problems cannot be ignored. These are realities and we should be concerned. However, we have to learn to separate the realities from the fantasies. We have to know what is real and what is a "what if."

It is also beneficial to develop a sense of acceptance. If I am worried about a situation I cannot control, I "turn it over to a higher power." This means I accept the situation as it exists, and go on with my business. I am not God. I cannot create miracles or change the flow of life. I tell myself "This is the situation that exists and I cannot do anything about it at this time. I therefore accept the situation and will wait and see what happens." This attitude allows me to use my energies in more beneficial ways and I do not boggle my mind with things I cannot do anything about anyway.

Guilt

Guilt gives us another reason to lay awake at night. If we can be objective, and not so hard on ourselves, we would realize that we have very little to feel guilty about. Realistically, we should only feel guilty about those things we have done intentionally to create hurt. The things that happen to others are not our responsibility and we have no real reason to feel guilty about them.

We, as agoraphobics, have been given a gift of sensitivity towards other people, and especially their feelings. This gift can be a blessing and a curse. It is a blessing because we are more aware of others needs and can help them. It is a curse because we have a tendency to put ourselves in their shoes, and feel what we think are their feelings.

Let us create a scenario:

You say something to your spouse and he or she reacts with a hurt look. You immediately feel guilty about saying it, even though it is something that must be said. You feel guilty for being honest and truthful with your feelings. You then apologize for saying it, and you are stuck with the feelings which have been denied or negated.

This can also be used as a weapon against you if the other person is aware you are going to react in this manner. It would be better for you and the other person to share the feelings in a non-threatening way and let him deal with it.

Guilt is a reasonable feeling when we have done something wrong and WE KNOW we have done something wrong. If you know you have not done anything wrong, and still feel guilty, it is an unreasonable feeling.

Another area of agoraphobic guilt is not being able to do something or be somewhere because of the limitations agoraphobia creates. It is a "damned if you do and damned if you don't" situation. Look at it this way. If you had a broken leg, would you be expected to do a certain thing or go to a certain place? Probably not. Of course, people can see the cast on your leg and will sympathize.

Agoraphobia is like having a "mental broken leg." Unfortunately, the cast cannot be seen, but it is there nevertheless. You are limited by the fears and "what if's." The feelings are real . . . as real as a broken leg. If we do what others want, and do it with anxiety, we feel guilty. If we don't do it, we feel guilty. And of what? We feel guilty for having a "broken leg." We did not intentionally break the leg. It happened to us and we have to deal with it. By feeling guilty, we are hampering our growth. I am aware that you cannot stop feeling guilty about certain things . . . but you can about some things. Separate the realities from the "what if's." Do not let guilt overwhelm you.

Resentment

This is another exercise that uses energy in a wasteful manner. Feelings of resentment have a way of festering and can grow into feelings of anger and hate. If you resent a person because they hurt you, wouldn't it make more sense to tell that person of your feelings, rather than hold it in and feel resentful? You resent your parents because of how they treated you when you were a child. What has been done has been done, and you cannot change the past. Why hold onto the resentment? Your husband or wife does not understand you, and you resent it. How can they understand you when you have difficulty understanding yourself? Can you see where this is leading?

Resentment is a negative attitude that only harms you and no one else. Don't you have enough problems in your life without adding resentment? Deal with resentment by affirming it is a waste of time, energy, and sleep and you do not need it in your life. Let go of it.

Accepting Your Feelings

All of the techniques I have written about and all of the advice I have given is meaningless unless you are willing to do one thing with your feelings, and that is, ACCEPT THEM. The most dangerous thing we can do is deny our true feelings. When we do this, we create a negative force within us that causes anxieties, physical symptoms, insecurities and lack of confidence. We become a walking steam kettle with no opening to release the pressure.

We do not have to accept everything that enters our lives. We deal with feeling problems as best we can. The problems of life that we have no control over, that frustrate us and cause feelings that we cannot do anything about, must be accepted and put to rest. Situations and circumstances can change at any time, and then we can deal with them.

There are good feelings as well as bad. When we are excited, the feelings are the same as those of being anxious. Yet, we accept the excitement. We even welcome it. This is because excitement is a positive force and anxiety is a negative. When we watch a sad program on television or read a sad book, we feel sad. And that is acceptable. However, when we feel depressed because of the circumstances of our lives, we make it unacceptable. Think about your reactions to your feelings and deal with them with reason and understanding.

Remember. . . .

Acceptance does not mean taking away free will or control.

You can choose what to accept and what not to.

Spend your time and energy on handling the realities in your life.

Separate the trees in the forest.

Stop being hard on yourself. Learn to love yourself.

Be good to yourself.

Use your energy towards attaining your recovery.

Use the power and courage within yourself to overcome any obstacles.

Make the choice whether you want your feelings to be your friend or enemy.

Deal with your negativity in a constructive, not destructive, manner.
Give yourself permission to be a happy, joyful person.
Above all, remember, YOU CAN DO IT!

Giving Yourself Permission to Be Human and Imperfect

6

Being aware that each of us is an individual, I avoid using the word "all" when referring to people. However, I feel confident in declaring that "*ALL* agoraphobics are perfectionists."

The agoraphobic's world is black or white. There's no gray. There is either passing or failing . . . zero or one hundred. There is only good or bad, right or wrong. They go through life with the attitude that "If I am not perfect, I am not acceptable." Because of this belief, they are constantly setting themselves up for disappointment.

This is an imperfect world. I am sure that if someone did invent the perfect mousetrap, someone else could come along and improve upon it by just moving a screw a sixteenth of an inch. I also feel that perfection is a bore. I prefer things that have a slight flaw. It gives them character. I feel that the handsomest star does not have the interesting facial characteristics of a person like Jack Klugman. Ingrid Bergman was more beautiful to me than the sexiest movie star we have today.

Agoraphobics, in their striving for perfection, lead a life of frustration, and are constantly asking themselves why they cannot accomplish their goals, whatever they may be. The reason is obvious. By expecting themselves to accomplish their goals perfectly, they are inevitably disappointed with the final results. This reinforces their feelings of inadequacy and affirms that they "cannot do anything right." They expect more of themselves than anyone else would expect of them. They tell themselves that "they can handle it" when they are not emotionally prepared or physically able to do so.

They create challenges in their lives that they are not ready to face . . . and then wonder why they have failed. If they successfully accomplish a goal, they negate the success by adding "but I had help" or "I didn't do it alone." Is it any surprise that when a challenge enters their lives, their first feelings are "I cannot do it." If they do not feel they can do it perfectly, it would not be acceptable or a real accomplishment.

A friend of mine was a functional agoraphobic and in the tour business. He was a perfectionist, always striving for the perfect tour. As a snack, champagne and a small basket of peanuts were served on the bus. One Saturday night he had what he thought was the perfect tour. Everything went well and all of the participants were happy about the wonderful evening they had . . . except one. He commented to my friend that the peanuts should be upgraded. This one single isolated comment destroyed his entire satisfaction with the tour. His constant, unrealistic striving for perfection was eventually his downfall and he gave up the business. His attitude to be perfect was his worst enemy. What a waste.

Why are agoraphobics perfectionists? The answer, like most other characteristics of the agoraphobic personality, goes back to our childhood. As I have explained in "Understanding Your Condition," we feel that no matter what we do, it is never enough. We are accustomed to having our best efforts rejected and negated. The subconscious message is, "If you want to be loved, you must be perfect." We take this belief with us into our adult lives. We still want to be loved and will be, only if we are perfect. The paradox is that we readily accept imperfection in others. We easily forgive them anything they may do or say. We justify their reasons for doing imperfect things. We forgive them even if we are hurt. We can be tolerant of them . . . but never of ourselves. If we were as hard on others as we are on ourselves, we would not have a friend left in the world.

We are people-pleasers. We will go out of our way to help others. We very rarely say a bad word about someone, although we may think it. We condone the behavior of others, constantly trying to "make everything nice." In a family dispute, we are always trying to make peace, no matter who is at fault. We straddle the middle of the fence, wanting everyone to like us, not hurting anyone. I sometimes think an agoraphobic should be Secretary of State. Perhaps then, we would have a peaceful world.

We want everyone to love us and will go to any length to secure that love. If someone rejects us, even slightly, we are devastated. Of course, we feel they are justified in their rejection of us, since we are not worthy anyway. They are right and we are wrong, no matter what the facts are. By being people-pleasers, we become victims. Better yet, we become "professional" victims, seeking out situations in which we can become involved with the hope that we can receive affirmation on "how wonderful we are."

Most agoraphobics I have spoken to tell me they are often sought out by friends as "dumping grounds", allowing them to unburden all of their troubles and problems on them. They are thought of as being so sensitive and wise. Actually, they are! Part of the agoraphobic personality is to be intuitively sensitive to other people's feelings and to be a good listener. They are sympathetic and can relate to peoples problems. When they offer advice, it is usually the non-threatening kind (peacemakers) and it is accepted by the other person because the advice usually does not have a risk involved. The agoraphobic listens patiently, while thinking, "What if this person knew what I am going through? Would they listen to me and understand?" But, we do not tell them. If we did, they would think of us as less than perfect.

Insights

The perfectionistic attitude created in our childhood stifles growth. *In order to grow emotionally, we must have a sense of accomplishment.* How can we have that feeling when everything we do does not meet our expectations of reaching perfection? We are defeated before we start. It may seem like a Catch–22 situation, one in which we cannot win. However, this is not true. The attitudes of perfectionism can be changed, just like any other attitude.

In order to identify your areas of perfectionism, I would like you to answer the following questions. Mark your degree of reaction by (1) if your reaction is strong, (2) if your reaction is mild, or, (3) if you do not have a reaction

1. Do you need to do things in as perfect a manner as possible?
2. Do you act impulsively?
3. Do you feel that your skills are limited, making you dependent on others to get things done?
4. Are you disillusioned when the behavior of others disappoints you?
5. When you are disappointed, or when things go badly, do you usually give up?
6. When you are frustrated, do you continue to make the same, unproductive responses?
7. Do you get upset when things do not go exactly as planned?
8. Do you try to accomplish too much too soon?

Analyze your answers to these questions. Do you notice a pattern? Are you easily disappointed in others? With yourself? Are you expecting too much of others? Of yourself? Are you setting yourself up for failure? Do you respond to disappointments in the same non-productive ways? There are many other questions you can ask yourself based on this small quiz. The insights are valuable, since they let us proceed with solutions.

It has been determined by Dr. Albert Ellis that three types of insights are necessary to change self defeating or perfectionistic behavior and reduce the intensity and number of upsets that you experience:

Insight number one: You must recognize and acknowledge that you have a problem and that past programming and events contributed to its development.

Insight number two: You must understand that most of your upsets and self defeating attitudes are caused by irrational " should/must" thinking that developed early in life and that these irrational thoughts are maintained by your continuous repetition of them to yourself. Actually, you work very hard on a conscious and subconscious level to maintain this type of irrational thinking.

Insight number 3: Having recognized the above insights, you fully ACCEPT the fact that the irrational "should/must" ideas that you have believed for so long are the basis for your upsets and self defeating behavior. Understanding this, you then recognize and *ACCEPT* that the only effective way of eliminating self defeating behavior and reducing the intensity and number of upsets in your life is to reprogram yourself to change the irrational "should/ must" thoughts and attitudes that produce them.

We tend to hold on to many strong beliefs that we may not be consciously aware of but are the basis for our inner thoughts, feelings and actions. This is due to the automatic response patterns that were discussed earlier and which enable us to take care of life's minor business without the need to consciously think about it. Unfortunately, when irrational beliefs are accepted and become part of this automatic response mechanism they tend to create self defeating behavior and upsets.

I am going to list ten most common irrational beliefs of this type as described by Dr. Ellis. While a person rarely has all ten of them, various combinations seem to cause many of the problems that we experience. We will examine each irrational belief and look at the thought process accompanying the belief, why the belief is irrational and ideas and thoughts you can use to overcome the belief. This will enable you to have an inner debate or what I call "self psyching" so that you can effectively challenge and deal with the irrational belief.

Irrational Belief Number One

I must feel loved and/or accepted for almost everything I do. (This belief is the result of an inner need for love and/or approval)

The Inner Thoughts:

I should not be irritable or unpleasant. (The need to always be pleasing to others)

He (she/they) should show me that he appreciates what I have done for him. (Usually accompanied by resentment when others don't show appreciation or at least recognition of things done for them)

I am not doing enough. I should do more. (A need to constantly do things for others and the feeling that you never do enough)

I must keep my husband (wife, children, others) happy. (The need to take responsibility for the happiness of others)

It is my fault they are upset. (Again, the need to take responsibility for happiness of others)

Why the Belief Is Irrational:

1. This belief is a perfectionistic, unattainable goal for three reasons:
    a. People around you will not be able, from time to time, to express love for *reasons that have nothing to do with you.*
    b. There are times when people around you will react negatively to things that you have done because of *their own* rational or irrational reasons.
    c. There is a certain percentage of people who won't like you because of *rational or irrational reasons of their own.*
2. In order to always feel loved, you must *always appear loveable and acceptable.* This is impossible.
3. You will always worry about *how much and how long* you will be loved.
4. You live your life for what you think others think and want to the *exclusion of your own needs.*
5. The greater your need for love and acceptance, the less people will care about you and respect you. This is because you will *tend to act in self defeating ways.*
6. You tend to become sensitive to any remark that you interpret as being unloving and this is an indication that the other person *does not love or approve of you.*
7. The need for love and approval expressed in this belief indicates your feelings of a *poor self image and worthlessness.*

Things to Do and Think:

1. Do what you really want to do rather that what people feel you should do.
    a. Ask yourself "What do I really want to do in this situation?"
    b. Avoid committing yourself at the spur of the moment. Take time to get in touch with your inner feelings.
2. Make the approval of others a desirable, but not necessary, goal.
3. Realize the difference between love and personal worth. This is especially necessary for those who had to do things to win approval in childhood.
4. Focus on loving rather than getting love.
5. Consider other peoples criticism of your actions objectively. If the criticism is unwarranted, do what is necessary. We all make mistakes. You are only human. Do not accept this as a negative evaluation of you as a person.

6. Work at improving your self image. Realize that you are a worthwhile person deserving of love.

Irrational Belief Number Two

I must be perfect.

The Inner Thoughts:

I must do this right. (Usually means perfectly)

I shouldn't be so stupid, clumsy, etc. (List of condemnations for shortcomings and mistakes)

If I don't do this right (perfect), I'm no good.

Why Belief Is Irrational:

1. No one can be totally masterful and competent in all aspects of their lives. Very few people display mastery and achievement in even one small area.
2. Perfection, by definition, is an impossible goal. We can only do our best.
3. Achieving your goals does not intrinsically relate to your worth as a person.
4. Trying to be perfect reflects a need to excel over others. Unfortunately, there is always someone who can do it better.
5. The need to attain perfection makes you anxious about failing. This prevents you from taking the risks necessary to attain recovery.

Things to Do and Think:

1. Every day do one thing for yourself that has no practical value. Just do it because you want to do it.
2. Give yourself permission to make a mistake. The world will not end.
3. Seek enjoyment in your tasks rather than accomplishment.
4. Attempt to "do well" rather than perfectly.
5. Work at bettering your own performance by practice and knowledge.
6. Do not delude yourself that you are a good or better person because you think you did something "perfectly."
7. Desire and work towards accomplishing your goals, but be ready to accept the possibility of failure.

Irrational Belief Number Three

When people act unfairly they are bad, wicked or rotten and they deserve severe blame or punishment. (This is usually based on the belief that a person's behavior determines their worth. It also tends to make a person excessively critical or judgmental)

The Inner Thoughts:

He/she is such a bad (evil, rotten etc.) person.

He/she is treating me unfairly and I should be treated fairly.

He/she is not doing it correctly (or right).

People should be different than the way they are.

Why Belief Is Irrational:

1. A person's behavior *always make sense to them* whether that behavior is rational or irrational.
2. Good and bad; fair and unfair; ethical and unethical are relative *terms that differ widely* according to place and circumstances.
3. In condemning others, you will *end up condemning yourself* if you do something "bad."
4. Because someone did a "bad" thing *does not mean that* they are bad.
5. When you blame others, you usually get angry or *hostile towards them.*
6. People who blame others (or themselves) are so afraid of making mistakes that *they will not take risks or make commitments to life.*

Things to Do and Think:

1. When you feel depressed or guilty, you can assume that you, on some level, are condemning yourself. You think. "I did this badly or wrongly and am therefore no good or worthless." Change your attitude to "I did not act in an appropriate way. Humans sometimes do this. How can I correct it next time?"
2. If you feel you did something unfairly, do what you can to correct the situation and ask forgiveness.
3. Distinguish between taking blame for your actions and being condemned for your actions.
4. Accept your own and others inappropriate behavior objectively. Human beings do not always act rationally.
5. Practice becoming more accepting of others short-comings.
6. Recognize that by being judgmental you perpetuate rather than correct their mistakes and yours.
7. Don't confuse a person with a deed. A person who acts badly on occasion may not be a bad person.

Irrational Belief Number Four

It is awful (terrible, horrible, catastrophic) when things do not go the way I would like them to go. (I am frustrated, treated unfairly, rejected, etc.) (This belief is characteristic of those with a tendency to exaggerate misfortunes and make little things into catastrophes)

The Inner Thoughts:

I cannot stand it when it happens.

Things should be different from the way they are.

That should not have happened.

If only . . .

Why the Belief Is Irrational:

1. While an event may be unpleasant, it is only catastrophic because you think of it that way.
2. If you make yourself upset by your frustrations and become depressed, you will block yourself from effectively removing them.
3. Accepting the reality of a situation gives you choices of either accepting it, changing it or leaving it alone.
4. Life will create situations and events that will create frustrations, whether we like it or not.

Things to Do and Think:

1. Determine whether an event or situation *contains true handicaps* or whether you have defined it as so.
2. Work at being able to accept things in a more *realistic way.*
3. If there is no way to change or control a frustrating event or situation, *accept it.*
4. Do what you can to change situations or events that you can have an affect on. If you cannot change them at this time, *wait patiently* for the time that you can change them.
5. Be aware that *frustrations are part of life.* They do not have to be turned into catastrophes.
6. You can view frustrations as undesirable, *but not as unbearable or intolerable.*

Irrational Belief Number Five

Emotional upsets and misery are the result of external pressures and causes and I have little or no ability to control or change my feelings. (Blaming other people, things or events for your upsets)

The Inner Thoughts:

That's just the way I am.

I can't help myself.

He (she, they, it) made me angry (anxious, sad, etc.)

Why the Belief Is Irrational:

1. Outside people and/or events cannot affect you unless you give them permission to affect you.
2. Frustrations are usually caused by your own irrational beliefs and expectations.
3. There are basically two kinds of pain, physical and psychological (mental). psychological pain is usually caused by:
   a. Your beliefs and attitudes about situations, events or people.
   b. You actually have more control over psychological pain than physical pain.
   c. Whenever you feel hurt or frustrated by someone else's words or deeds, you are giving them a power that they don't possess. You can only hurt yourself.

Things to Do and Think:

1. Realize that it is *your own irrational thinking* and your constant repetition of it that is creating you problems. Proper re-programing can change this.
2. Work at discovering your "should/must" script and *replacing your child-like reactions* with realistic preferences.
3. When faced with emotional criticisms from others, *question the motives* of those that criticize and the truth of the statements.
   a. If the criticism is warranted, work at changing your behavior or accept your own limitations.
   b. If the criticism is unwarranted, accept the fact that people are often irrational and dismiss it.

Irrational Belief Number Six

If something seems threatening (whether real or unreal), I must preoccupy myself with it and become upset about it.

(This belief is characteristic of people who spend a tremendous amount of time and energy worrying about things (whether real or unreal) and focusing on the negative aspects of their lives.)

The Inner Thoughts:

What if . . . ? (Negative reaction)

It was good except for . . . (Denial)

I did OK but . . . (Denial)

I should get upset (It shows I care)

Why the Belief Is Irrational:

1. If something actually seems threatening (real or unreal) there are only two rational approaches:
   a. Do something practical to alleviate the threat,

      or
   b. If you cannot do anything, accept its existence.
2. Worrying about it does not change the happening.
3. You assume that a potentially unpleasant event can be catastrophic.
4. Worry itself is a most painful condition.
5. You do have control and can change most unpleasant situations. If you cannot, you must accept them for the time being.

Things to Do and Think:

1. *Seriously question the real danger* of the things you fear and determine if they will actually occur without a doubt or if they will lead to catastrophes.
   a. When the situation actually involves threat, do what is practical to change the situation or accept it.
   b. Seriously weigh the chances of the situation actually occurring.
2. Life contains certain *inevitable* threats and risks.
3. Most of your over-concern stems from *irrational thinking.*
4. Most anxieties are related to *making public mistakes* (a fool of yourself) or the possible loss of love and acceptance. Question the reality of your condition.
5. Worrying about many situations will *aggravate* them rather than improve them.
6. Try not to exaggerate the *importance* of material things.
7. Present fears are usually based on earlier origins and *do not apply to you today.* They are no longer appropriate.
8. Change "what if . . ." statements to *"So what if. . .".*
9. *Do not deny* successes or other good things in your life.
10. *Accept your feelings.*

Irrational Belief Number Seven

It is easier to avoid facing many of life's difficulties and responsibilities than it is to face them. (This belief is often characteristic of those that have a fear of failure and/or to take risks)

The Inner Thoughts:

It's just too difficult for me.

I'll just ignore it and it will go away.

I don't want to think about it.

You decide.

Why the Belief Is Irrational:

1. Avoidance usually leads to discomfort afterwards (guilt, worry)
2. Avoidance decreases self confidence and esteem.
3. Avoiding making a decision is in itself a decision.

Things to Do and Think:

1. Change short-range gratifications to long-range, *more gratifying goals.*
2. *Use self discipline* to attain the goals that are necessary or desirable for happiness and fulfillment. Dedicate yourself to attaining the goal.
3. Use extra push and energy *to get started* towards your goals.
4. Use a *schedule or program* to attain goals. Set sub-goals.
5. Be *patient* in attaining goals. *Do not be hard on yourself.*

Irrational Belief Number Eight

The past is of utmost importance because, once something strongly influences your life, it will always determine your feelings and behavior today.

(Holding on to the past gives you reasons to remain the way you are)

The Inner Thoughts:

I've always been this way.

You can't teach an old dog new tricks.

If only I could do it all over again, things would be different.

I wish I could do it all over again so things could be different.

Why the Belief Is Irrational:

1. Because you once felt a certain way does not mean you will always feel that way.
2. Strong influences of past events stifles growth into the future.
3. Behavior appropriate at one time may be inappropriate at other times.
4. Performing things the same way you did in the past may be the cause of your failures today.
5. The present is not the same as the past. All things are different.

Things to Do and Think:

1. Accept the fact that your past does influence you in some ways while accepting the fact that *the present is where you now live.*

2. Consider your past history objectively so that you can *learn from the past mistakes.*

3. Work at changing the present so that you can *create a better tomorrow.*

4. Realize that *your past has passed.*

Irrational Belief Number Nine

People should be, and things should happen, differently. (This belief is frequently a characteristic of people with perfectionistic attitudes)

The Inner Thoughts:

He (she, they, it) shouldn't be like that.

I can't stand not knowing how to do this (or do it "right")

I just can't seem to find the answer or solution (meaning "perfect" solution)

I should have acted differently.

Why It Is Irrational:

1. No reason exists why people or events "should" turn out any better than they do.

2. If, in the past, you knew a specific action would have produced a better result, you would have taken that action. The reality is that you did not know.

3. When people behave, or, events take place in a way you do not like, it is your reaction that creates the negative effect.

4. You cannot control the behavior of others.

5. The idea of an absolutely right or perfect solution to any problem is not probable since most problems usually have many possible solutions.

6. Few things are "black or white." Most things fall into the gray areas of life.

Things to Do and Think:

1. Ask yourself if you should *really be affected* by someone else's "bad" or inappropriate behavior.
    a. Do you really care what this person does?
    b. Do their actions truly affect you?
    c. Will this person change?

2. Adopt a permissive, uncritical attitude towards others.

3. Work on focusing on what you do (your actions) rather than on the actions of others.

4. Since no perfect solutions exist, accept compromises and reasonable solutions.

Irrational Belief Number Ten

I get my happiness by being inactive or "passively" taking it easy and enjoying myself.

(This belief is a common rationalization of those who have a fear of failure and/or believe that it is dangerous to take risks)

The Inner Thoughts:

It is easier to just not face it.

It's too much effort and trouble.

Nothing seems to interest me.

That all seems so boring. I'd rather not do anything.

Why the Belief Is Irrational:

1. People rarely feel happy or alive when they are not participating in life.

2. Most people require absorbing activities to be happy in life.

3. People who lead a passive existence usually have a fear of failure.

Things to Do and Think:

1. Be involved with and absorbed by life. These should be *involvements that truly interest you and will bring you self approval and gratification*.

   a. Loving other people (rather than desiring to get love)

   b. Creating things to be absorbed in.

   c. Becoming absorbed in ideas and future projections.

2. When getting involved in an endeavor of choice, choose a *challenging long-range one* rather than simple or short-ranged one.

By recognizing these irrational beliefs which affect your life, you can accomplish changes that are necessary to achieve recovery from agoraphobia. Remember, recovery is not attained only by relief of the anxiety symptoms, but also by changing the old belief system into a new, more positive one. You must release the past before you can go into the future.

Negative Anticipation 7

Various forms of negative anticipation have been discussed in previous chapters and how it affects our feelings and physical condition, creates scenarios in our subconscious and limits our functioning.

It is important to understand the "why's" of negative anticipation. It is not a phenomena exclusive to agoraphobics. Everyone has a tendency to think negatively on occasion. It is not unusual for someone feeling ill to think the worse, or having a chest pain to think of the possibility of a coronary. Not is it unusual for a person anticipating a conflict to think negatively upon the outcome. We all revert back to childhood fears when faced with unpleasant or threatening situations. So you see, negative anticipation is more common, and perhaps, normal than we think.

However, we agoraphobics, being over-reactors, take the negative thought to it's zenith. It's what I refer to as "action vs. reaction vs. over-reaction." We are all familiar with the "thought creating fear creating anxiety" cycle discussed earlier. What I want to concentrate on is the thought. Usually a negative thought on either the conscious or the subconscious level is the first step in the "fear cycle." Let us create a scenario:

Uncle John has died and you are expected to attend the wake and funeral. You know if you don't, the family (not understanding your condition) would be very angry. However, you feel that if you do go, the experience will create much anxiety and perhaps, panic.

This is the beginning of the "fear cycle" and you start to create the negative scenario. As time passes the scenario becomes more and more real in your mind and you become more frightened at the prospect. You start thinking of excuses not to go. As the hour of commitment grows closer, the fear and negative anticipation become stronger.

Your sleep is affected because the fearful thoughts are dominating your mind. You become overwhelmed and confused because you do not feel you have an "out." The scenario becomes even more vivid in your mind and you are adding more fears to the original fear.

You do not feel you can discuss your feelings with anyone because they will not understand and might force you to make a firm commitment to go. It seems like a "no-win" situation. If you do not go, the family will be angry. If you do go, you fear that you will experience anxiety and perhaps make a fool of yourself. What to do?

All of us have gone through situations similar to this. Usually the fear overwhelms us and we do not go. We then feel all of the guilt created by the "failure" and condemn ourselves for being "weak." We cannot *accept our decision* not to go, but nurture our feelings of failure by internal thoughts such as "I should have been able to go" or "Everyone else went . . . why couldn't I?" We go round and round justifying a terrible dilemma we have created for ourselves.

When I refer to "action vs. reaction vs. over-reaction" I am referring to situations which occur in our lives and how we handle them. We did not expect Uncle John's death, and yet, here it is and we are involved. This is the "action." Our initial negative anticipation and the fearful thoughts are the "reaction." Then we take the situation to it's pinnacle and convinced ourselves that it would be impossible to attend the wake and funeral. This is the "over-reaction." If, at sometime between the reaction and over-reaction, we could objectively look at the situation and could consider the options open to us, perhaps the end result would have been different. Let's explore the possibilities:

1. You would not be alone attending the wake or funeral. Relatives, support people and others who are aware that you have some sort of a problem would also be there. Think of the one who would be most understanding and ask if they would help you through this time by being close by in case they were needed. Just having the knowledge that help is close would alleviate much of the anxiety.

2. Being emotionally upset is "normal" at a time like this. You would not be thought of as strange if you are "nervous."

3. You cannot *really predict* how you would feel if you attended. You *THINK* you would feel anxious and perhaps panic.

4. Historically, agoraphobics function well when others need them. Your own fears would probably be put aside when comforting others.

5. You know that it would be better to face the event than to face angry relatives.

6. If you are taking medication, this is the time it is put to it's best use. Use it as prescribed by your doctor.

7. It is the child within you that is fearful. Call upon the adult within you to face this situation.

8. Prepare yourself by practicing your relaxation techniques.

Perhaps what I have outlined above may not seem possible to some of you. You have convinced yourself that there is no way that you would be able to attend Uncle John's funeral. It is too fearful. Let me reassure you. It *is* possible. You just think it is impossible. Weigh the pro's and con's. Determine whether it is worth the risk.

The pro's are:

If you go, you will not reap the anger of the family.

You will feel better about yourself.

You "should" be there.

You have experienced anxiety and panic before . . . and survived.

The con's are:

You might panic; You might panic; You might panic; You might panic.

However, have you ever thought of the possibility that you might *NOT* panic.

If you prepare yourself properly, you might be able to attend and feel comfortable. You don't really know, do you? If you do not allow the fear and irrational thoughts to overwhelm you, you might be able to do it. Think about it. Weigh the pro's and con's and then make a firm decision.

If you decide not to go, realize that this is *your* decision and do not allow yourself to feel guilty about it. That's the way it is. If you decide to go, then think positively about it. Do all that necessary to take on the challenge and know that you are properly prepared.

When we go through the process of negative anticipation, we experience inappropriate feelings. They are exaggerated and self defeating. These feelings are usually the result of irrational beliefs and expectations. Irrational beliefs and expectations are almost always characterized by the words "should", "must" and "ought." When your mind is locked into the traps these words create, possibilities of words such as "want", "need" and "desire" are locked out.

You mull endlessly about catastrophic results. You convince yourself that you cannot do anything about it. The realities of "should" or "must" situations are:

They are used as absolutes. There are *no absolutes* in the real world.

They prevent you from considering the possibilities of *options*.

They always *create anxiety*.

The "should's" or "must's" are usually created by someone else's in-put. "*They*" are saying you should or must.

71

The "should's" or "must's" that you are dealing with now stem from your childhood. It is Mommy or Daddy saying you should or must. Your desire to please them is transferred to trying to please everyone. We find it very difficult to say "No." In order to overcome this self defeating thought process, we must think more like an adult. This means being more realistic and rational. Rational thinking helps you in making decisions that are best suited to you and leads to a more pleasurable, enjoyable and worthwhile life.

Eliminate conflicts before they can affect you.

Consider your assets and liabilities.

Remember, there are the things you can do, the things you can't do and the things *YOU THINK* you can't do. They must all be put into their proper places in your thinking and accomplishing goals.

You have beliefs and expectations about life. Then, when a life experience occurs, (such as Uncle John's death) an *interpretation* is made based on your beliefs and expectations, (action). Your interpretation generates a feeling that causes you to respond in some way (reaction). Then, of course, we proceed to the "over-reaction".

As agoraphobics, we tend to immediately react by thinking we CAN'T do it. Before making that decision, consider doing the following:

Weigh the options available to you.

Try not to reach a firm decision until all the possibilities are explored.

Think of the pro's and con's of the situation.

Think in positive ways. Ask yourself "What is it I have to do?" Then do what you can to develop a plan to deal with it.

Eliminate negative self-statements.

Think rationally.

Say "So What" to the "What Ifs".

Rather than defeating yourself with the thought of "I can't," think "I choose not to" and that's OK.

Whatever situation or events come into your life, the world will not end if you do not fulfill the "should's" or "must's."

If you feel you can accomplish the goal, take it one step at a time.

Don't let the goal overwhelm you.

Deal with the here and now, not what you fantasize might be.

You cannot predict the future.

Think of how good you will feel when you accomplish the goal.

Feel and know that you can deal with any situation or event that comes into your life, if you choose to.

Use all the "tools" available to you.

All agoraphobics have an inner strength that, when called upon, can see them through the worse of adversities. Have faith in yourself.

Set-backs

One of the major concerns, and therefore, negative anticipations of recovering agoraphobics is the fear of setbacks. This is one of the most common calls we receive at the New Beginning Foundation.

The person calling has been doing well and feeling better and taking more risks and having successes. Suddenly, as if from out of the blue, they have an anxiety attack. The attack frightens them and they feel that they are going backwards to where they were before they were feeling well.

There are many reasons for set-backs. The most common is the resistance of that part of your subconscious (the child) wanting to hold on the agoraphobia and "sabotaging" the growth process. I have written previously about the child within us that creates the agoraphobic symptoms and fears. That "child" dominates the emotional part of us when we are fearful and anxious. That "child" is an insecure, fearful child and when it dominates our emotional being it makes us feel fearful, anxious, stressful, inadequate and insecure.

These feelings create the physical symptoms we know so well. When we are doing well we must remember that, the "child" within is waiting for the opportunity to negate all that we have accomplished. This is not a conscious action, but a subconscious one.

When we become vulnerable by situations entering our lives which creates "normal" stress or anxiety, or, an illness, or, just becoming lax and not reinforcing our positive attitudes, the "child" within us will again attempt to send the messages of fear. What must be learned is not to react to those messages. Tell yourself that "It is just the child within me and he/she can be ignored." Remember, it is not the message, but the reaction to the message that creates the anxiety attacks.

When an attack comes, we are taken by surprise. Our old fears are rekindled and we doubt ourselves and our successes. "They were only temporary," we think. This is not true. It is not a step backwards. You could compare it with having a sudden muscle spasm or headache. It will pass.

The problems arise by our reaction and over-reaction to the attack, not the attack itself. We become fearful when the attack occurs and start the fear to anxiety to self doubt to more fear cycle. If we allow this cycle to proceed, the old symptoms start to reoccur. Break the cycle at its onset as previously discussed.

Continue going forward and renew your attitudes and positive thinking.

You are in control. Never forget that.

Continue giving yourself positive affirmations such as, "I am in control of my feelings," "This will soon pass," "The child within me is just showing off," "I am not afraid," "I am an adult and will react like an adult."

Learn not to over-react.

Remain calm as possible and "flow" through it.

If we allow ourselves to become overwhelmed and fearful, we become ineffective.

Be patient with yourself.

Set-backs are opportunities to learn. We do not learn from successes. They are simply affirmations of what we are capable of accomplishing when we are ready. We learn from our failures and set-backs. We can evaluate our reactions and over-reactions and develop better ways of dealing with them and make the proper adjustments. Whether you are agoraphobic or not, things are not always going to go the way you want them to. In order to recover it is necessary to learn to deal with these times in a positive and affirmative manner. We have discussed many useful techniques and new attitudes to deal effectively with these types of situations. If you will use them, you will find they will work.

Relating

Another area which creates negative anticipation is our tendency to relate to what we think other's are feeling. In other words, we put ourselves, on a feeling level, in other people's shoes. If we have to say something unpleasant or critical, we start to think of how we would feel if it was said to us and how we would react. We then think the other person is going to feel or react in the same way. If we really had the power of knowing how the other person would feel or react, we could become millionaires. Any advertising agency would be anxious for our services. The reality is that there isn't any way that you can know or anticipate how others will feel or react.

You think, "If this was said to me, I would feel a certain way and the other person would feel the way I feel." Nothing can be further from the truth. Their feelings and reactions are very individual. They cannot feel your feelings and you cannot feel theirs. By negatively anticipating what they may feel, you stifle yourself and do not allow your true feelings to be known.

It has been my experience in helping others attain recovery that the negative anticipation is one of the last things to leave the agoraphobic personality. This is due to the years invested in thinking in this manner and it is a hard habit to break.

What is more important than the negative anticipation is the reaction to it. When you are on your road to recovery, you must ignore the childlike thinking created by the "What If's" and do what must be done in spite of the message. When you have attained confident and positive attitudes, this is not difficult.

Keep reminding yourself that the negativity is created by the emotionally fearful, insecure child but you can deal with your life as an adult. The more often you do this, the less the child will send these irrational fears into your thoughts.

Be patient with yourself and keep working towards accomplishing your goals.

The road to recovery is not a smooth one, but with perseverance and faith you can complete the journey.

Confidence and Self Esteem

8

As a teenager, I recall having feelings of being "different." My friends seemed much more outgoing and easy going. Things they seemed able to do with confidence, I found to be difficult. I avoided competitive sports believing I wasn't good enough and I feared making a fool of myself in front of my friends. Challenges that would seem normal to a teenager, such as meeting girls or going to parties, I carefully avoided. Although comfortable in a crowd, I could not handle one-on-one confrontations.

Being a creative "teenage agoraphobic," I learned to make adjustments so that I could be accepted by my peers and avoid threatening or challenging situations. I became a "people pleaser." I learned early in life that people loved to talk to others about their troubles and concerns, so I became a good listener. People liked you when you made them laugh, so I memorized jokes and developed a sense of humor. By using these learned skills, I was accepted. I did not know that my problem stemmed from feelings of insecurity and low self confidence. All I knew was that I felt "different."

As a mature person, well past my "agoraphobic career," I still have my sense of humor and the ability to listen well. However my needs to be liked and accepted by others have changed. The major difference between myself as a teenager and myself as an adult is that I really *like* me now. During my research of agoraphobia, I realized how vital that change was in my recovery. My low self esteem and lack of confidence had contributed greatly in keeping me in the agoraphobic state.

In a previous chapter I stated that *ALL* agoraphobics are perfectionists. I now state that *ALL* agoraphobics suffer from low levels of confidence and self esteem. The fearful, emotionally insecure child within you is dominating your emotional personality. This child does not have high levels of confidence and self esteem and as a result agoraphobics find this lack to be part of their emotional make-up.

To compensate for this, we become "people-pleasers" and over-achievers. Some interesting case histories of agoraphobic over-achievers are Howard Hughes and Sigmund Freud. You might be surprised to learn that these people were agoraphobic. Read their biographies and determine for yourselves. Imagine being as much in demand as they were, and still dealing with the extreme stress of agoraphobia. And yet, it is no different for us. Each situation . . . each event . . . each challenge . . . creating feelings of doubt and making us feel that we are not capable.

I recently received the following letter. It is a perfect example of the development of a child that has feelings of low self esteem and confidence into an adult still experiencing the same feelings:

CASE HISTORY—JANE

Dear Mr. Green,

Thank you so very much for sending me the tapes and the reading materials. I cried when I read "Understanding Your Condition". No one has explained it the way you did.

My childhood was, to put it mildly, horrid. My dad died when I was six years old and eleven months later my mom was found to have T.B. and was put into a sanitarium. We kids (there was six of us) were put into foster homes where we were beaten, sexually abused and starved. I had always been a timid child and in these homes I became worse. I became a "good girl" who did exactly as I was told, but my best was never good enough. We were constantly told how stupid we were, how lazy and dirty. Everything to rob us of our self esteem and confidence. I always felt I didn't belong, unloved and completely without self worth. And what is strange is that everyone always said what a great attitude I had. I was always smiling. I never showed my feelings. I was like that song "Laughing on the outside, crying on the inside". I stifled every emotion. If we cried when we were beaten or scolded, we were beaten again . . . so we learned early not to cry.

This happened for 10 years from age 6 to 16. I still find it very hard to let out my feelings. Of the six of us I am the only one that is agoraphobic. My brothers drink a great deal and when they do they cry about their lost childhood. But I notice they only talk about it when they are drinking . . . almost like it is to painful to talk about when they are sober.

I also married a super critical man who in a minute can make me feel stupid and inadequate.

I cried again when I heard you say that agoraphobics are courageous people and every time I hear it I cry. No one ever said that to me although I worked and did many things while having anxiety attacks. I blamed them on hypoglycemia. But in the last part of 1982 they became worse and worse until in

1983 (March) I had to quit my job because I felt like I was going to die. The anxiety became sheer panic.

By the way, I was denied my Social Security benefits or S.S.I. because the psychiatrist they sent me to said "So you're afraid of crowds. Well, you can work in a place where you can be alone." I was so close to panic and my mind was just on the fear of what was going to happen I didn't argue with him. All I wanted was to get out of his office.

I am using the tapes faithfully. I want more than anything to get over this agoraphobia and get on with my life. I haven't any support from my family. My husband says I could get over it if I wanted to. I am just using it to get attention and my children don't even want to hear about it. I think they are ashamed of their mother's condition. But you see, I don't tell people about it either except a couple of friends who I knew would understand. I'm sure most people, if they knew, would think I was crazy.

God bless you, Mr. Green. And again, thank you.

Sincerely, Jane . . .

I feel much compassion for Jane and the many others who have shared their stories with me. I have faith that I will be able to help her attain her dream of "going on with her life." Many others whose backgrounds were as devastating as Jane's have recovered and she will too.

Low self esteem and lack of confidence are not exclusive to agoraphobics and there are many "normal" people who have the same feelings. Many of those so called "normal" people use agoraphobics as "dumping grounds" because we are such "towers of strength." If they only knew! We listen attentively . . . we make them laugh . . . and all the time we are cringing inside, hoping that they do not see through us. Do not be concerned. They won't. We are the "masters of disguise."

We are always comparing ourselves to others (*they* always being better) and affirming our limitations (*they* can always do it better). These comparisons confirm our beliefs that we are not as good as others. We have developed this trait of comparing in our early childhood. Our parents, ("Why aren't you like your cousin?"), our teachers, ("You could get A's like Mary."), our peers, ("I want Johnny on our team, not you.") and then finally, from ourselves ("I'm a born loser.") This programing becomes our own beliefs which help keep us limited in dealing with life's situations. Since we are products of our own unique life experiences, how can we realistically compare ourselves with anyone else.

Self esteem stems from your concepts about yourself or, your belief system. It can also be described as your "life script." This script affects your successes and failures, your hopes and desires, your moods and your actions. Your life script is created in your childhood. Life script messages usually start with the word "don't." Messages such as "Don't think" (usually affecting women), "Don't feel" (usually affecting men), "Don't be important" (Who do you think you are?) affect our future lives. Repetitive statements by parents such as

"You'll never grow up to be anything" affirm our feelings of low self esteem. Self esteem is the same as self concept. Your conception of yourself dictates the world's concept of you.

One of the biggest misconceptions is that we should love others *more* than we should love ourselves. If we do not put their needs and desires before ours, we think of ourselves as *selfish*. As we learned in early childhood, being selfish means being "bad." Mommy says "Give sister the candy or you are being selfish." The fact that it is your candy and you don't want to share it with your sister has nothing to do with it. If you don't do it, "you're selfish." If you do give the candy to your sister, you are left in a confused state. You were not "selfish" and gave her the candy, but you still feel bad. Since you feel that way you must actually be "bad." This is the way a child will think. As agoraphobic adults we think and feel the same way.

Consider an alternative way of thinking of yourself when you feel you are being "selfish". You can think of being selfish as having feelings of *self love*. You love yourself enough to do what is good and beneficial for *you*. This does not mean that you do not consider others. It means that you evaluate a situation and consider your needs *first*. If you wish to fill another's needs, you do it by choice, not because, if you do not, you are being "selfish." Having the choice gives you value. Only by knowing that you have value will you be able to be of value to others.

You are unique. Accept yourself for who and what you are. There never was another "you" and never will be. When you create change, do so because you want to be the best you not because you want to be like someone else. You need high levels of self esteem and confidence to grow out of agoraphobia. Improving your levels of self esteem and confidence must have top priority in your recovery plan.

Your life script can be changed. Here are some suggestions on how to accomplish this:

Changing Life Scripts

Learn to release the past and deal with the present.

If your "here and now" is positive and affirmative, your future will also be.

You cannot change what happened years, days or even minutes ago.

It is only the "now" that really matters.

Many of my clients get locked into the past and, by doing this, create reasons to hold on to their limitations ("Don't blame me. See what my mother did when I was a child.") Reasons can easily be turned into excuses and excuses justify actions. The past has minor importance in your life. Compare it to the present and the future since these direct the life you are going to live from this moment forth.

There comes a time in our lives when we must reach what I call "ground zero". This is a dividing line between the past and the future when you must say to yourself "Anything in the past that is not positive, affirmative or beneficial to me, I release. From this day forward, I will deal with my present in positive ways and with positive attitudes. There is nothing that I could do now to change what has happened in the past, and so, I release it." When this statement becomes your belief, you will be free of the past and it's limiting hold on you.

Say good things about yourself and your attributes *often*. Do this whenever you can. If you do not have the opportunity to say them out loud, think them.

If you read a poem or a saying or any other printed matter that you relate to in a positive way, cut it out and hang it in a place you look at often. A bathroom mirror or a refrigerator door is ideal. Stop and read it often.

When you think negatively about yourself, form the habit of counteracting the negative with a positive thought. It can even be silly, such as "I may be fat, but I don't sweat much." Get into the habit of doing this.

Use mental imagery. This means seeing yourself, in your imagination, as a totally functional, normal human being. Imagine that you are looking at a movie screen. Imagine yourself on the screen doing the things you want to do, feeling good about yourself, being calm and comfortable. Act out any situations you wish with successful conclusions. Do verbal interplays with others by seeing them on the screen with you. This process deals directly with the subconscious mind and can be even more effective if you learn techniques of self hypnosis.

Maintain a positive attitude towards others. What you give is what you receive.

Give compliments frequently and freely. They make others feel better, and, in turn, make you feel better. It also makes others feel better about *you*.

Avoid, if you can, those in your life who are always negative. Ongoing discussions about sickness, bad breaks, the unfairness of life and all of that other garbage should not have any place in your life. This type of input nurtures your own negative feelings and justifies your low self esteem and confidence.

Train yourself to think positively and optimistically. Think thoughts such as "I would rather be in this world, as bad as others think it is, than not be in it. My future lies ahead of me and I am going to have a positive future as a totally normal, functional person."

Become optimistically realistic about your world and yourself. An old saying that I use is that the Black Hole of Calcutta was easy to heat. You can find positive things about most situations. Focus on that, not the negative.

You can believe in Santa Claus or the Tooth Fairy if you wish, but also believe in yourself.

Have faith in the human race.

Reward yourself for the good things you do and for the good person you are. You don't have to reward yourself with a gold piece of jewelry. A pint of Baskin-Robbins ice cream can go a long way in making you feel good.

Make a list of your good qualities and your bad. I'm willing to bet that, if you are honest, the good quality list will be the longer one. Then, throw away the bad list.

Subconscious re-programing is very useful in changing attitudes about yourself. This technique is used extensively at the New Beginning Foundation. Self hypnotic procedures are used in this process although there are other ways to reprogram oneself. Repetition of a message consciously that will penetrate the subconscious is a proven method used by the advertising industry. The message is repeated and repeated and before you know it, you are buying chocolate covered ants. You have been programmed to believe that your life is not complete unless you have chocolate covered ants. The message becomes a subjective truth.

You can use this process with the use of audio cassettes, particularly motivating ones. I attribute much of my recovery to listening to audio cassettes created by a motivational speaker named Zig Zigler. I played and replayed his cassettes often during my recovering stage. This positive input helped me in overcoming the negativity I felt and I used it often in getting through many difficult times. Reading and re-reading motivational and inspiring books can also aid in feeling more confident.

I know that you have tried many of the techniques discussed and perhaps they didn't seem to work for you. This is because you expect a book or a tape to do it for you. It doesn't work that way. You have to take action to support the positive input. Remember, you want to change your belief system, one that you have had for many years. This takes time and dedication. It takes work!

It also means that you have to use your creative imagination, the one thing that all agoraphobics have. Use it constructively, not destructively. The same imagination that we use to create the negative scenarios which cause our limitations can be used to create the positive attitudes and belief system that means high levels of self confidence and esteem.

The way to change is to start *NOW!*

Fear and Risk 9

Agoraphobia has been referred to as the "fear of a fear" or a "phobia-phobia." I have defined agoraphobia as the "fear of the anxiety that might lead to panic." This definition further identifies the "fear of a fear". The first fear is the feeling of anxiety that can lead to the second fear, which is the fear of having a panic attack.

This "fear of a fear" attitude is not uncommon, even amongst non-agoraphobics. A person going to the doctor because of constant headaches could fear (first) the headaches and (second) that it could be caused by a brain tumor. Even more common might be the strange noise in an automobile engine. First fear . . . there is something wrong. Second fear . . . it is serious and might cost a lot of money to repair. This type of anticipatory fear is irrational since it has no basis in fact. However, irrational or not, the mind works in peculiar ways.

The subconscious mind, which creates the feelings associated with the thought, does not discern between rational or irrational conscious thoughts. The reaction to the "fear of a fear" input creates the feelings of insecurity, doubt and a sureness that the worst will happen. It is the feelings, not the logical reality, that creates the problems that we react to.

Because of their low self concept, agoraphobics react differently to these feelings. The confident person, faced with the problem of headaches, might have thought of a more serious cause, but will go to the doctor with the belief that it can be treated and he will be cured. The agoraphobic will resist facing the reality and avoid the doctor, being sure that he will find what is feared . . . the dreaded brain tumor. He will suffer in fear, each reoccurrence of the headache assuring him that he is going to die. Is it any wonder that this constant input of fearful, negative anticipation creates physical symptoms that affirm the seriousness of the condition.

It is a repeat of the "thought to fear to anxiety to more fear to more anxiety" cycle that eventually leads to the panic. The confident person reacts . . .

the agoraphobic reacts and then over-reacts. Again, it is the over-reaction that is the real problem.

We must remember that fear is a normal and necessary emotion. Without it, civilization would never have survived. Fear, in itself, is a positive, not a negative. It kept the caveman in his cave in times of danger. It keeps us from stepping into heavy traffic. There are many levels of fear, as in physical fear (I am going to be attacked by a lion) and psychological fear (I *think* I am going to be attacked by a lion).

Most of us, agoraphobic or not, will react appropriately to the physical fear. We will take proper action to prevent the event from happening. We can run, we can hide or we can get a gun and shoot the lion. We can generally handle it. It is the psychological fear that we have difficulty with. Since it is a "might happen," we can only guess what preventative measures to take.

In the case of the agoraphobic, since the fantasy created is a negative one and he is sure the worst is going to happen, the options become limited. The subconscious does not discern between fantasy and reality, and the reaction is going to be based on the negative input. The result . . . anxiety to fear to more anxiety, etc.

The basis for this thought process goes back to child-hood programing, as do all other childlike emotions experienced by the agoraphobic. Rational or irrational, real or unreal, right or wrong, has nothing to do with it. The basic mistake most therapists and others make when dealing with the agoraphobic, is that they feel a logical explanation will change the fearful feelings. They can use all of the logic in the world, but be assured, the fearful feelings being felt by the agoraphobic will not go away. Feelings must be dealt with on a feeling, not logical, level.

When the agoraphobic is irrationally fearful, they are childlike. They must be comforted and reassured, not lectured to. Logic denies their feelings. Intellectually, or consciously, they know they are not being rational, but this knowledge does not take away the feelings of fear. Fear is an emotion and must be dealt with as such.

The husband that tells his agoraphobic wife that she is foolish to feel fear when he thinks there is nothing to fear is denying her feelings, and making her feel even more insecure. Instead of helping, he is harming. Feelings of fear do not have to be rational or real in his eyes. The important thing is that she is feeling the fear and that is the reality. The husband does not have to understand *why* she is fearful, he has to accept that *she is* and react appropriately.

If he were dealing with a 6 year old child who was afraid of a ghost in the closet, he would accept this fear as "normal." He would calm the child by holding her and telling her that he will protect her. He will comfort the child and do all that is necessary to make the child feel more secure. This is the reaction to the fear that the agoraphobic wife needs. If this is done, rather than the denial of her feelings, the fear would soon pass.

Unfortunately, it is difficult for the husband to relate to his wife as a "child" and himself as the protective, nurturing "father" figure. There are times in all of our lives when we revert to "children." All of us, when we are threatened, become "fearful children" and want to be reassured. It is a matter of degree and frequency. The agoraphobic needs more reassurance than non-agoraphobics. Low self confidence, low self esteem, low self concept are the basis for their problems, and it is shown in their fearful reactions and over-reactions.

The belief that nurturing this type of irrational fear will only make the agoraphobic more dependent is false. A child that is comforted and reassured does not become more dependent. She becomes more secure and confident. This has been proven in many research projects. It is a necessary part of a child's emotional growth and is a necessary part of an agoraphobics growth.

I have labeled many of the fears felt by agoraphobics as "irrational." This is a true statement, but is misleading. Rational and irrational can only apply to the person experiencing the fear. What might seem irrational to one person could be absolutely rational to another.

Let's create a scenario:

A very common fear among agoraphobics is that of being alone.

Harry (the husband) wants to go to a ball game and Mary (the wife and agoraphobic) does not feel she can go because of the agoraphobic fears and "what if's." She asks Harry not to go . . . not to leave her alone. Harry's reaction is "Nothing is going to happen. I will only be gone a couple of hours. You are safe in your own home." He feels her fears and request are irrational. Logic prevails. He is focusing on a physical danger to Mary and feels confident that nothing will happen to her. He cannot understand why she feels the way she does. He cannot relate.

Mary is feeling . . . "If I am left alone, I will not have anyone close by to help me if I feel anxious and panic. The panic might get so bad that I will get hysterical and the fear will overwhelm me. I can see myself running through the house screaming and no one will be there to help me. I could have a stroke or heart attack and I will be alone."

To Mary, these thoughts are very real. To her, these feelings of fear are rational. All of the logic that Harry uses to try to make Mary more comfortable about his going to the ball game will not work. The feelings of fear are too overwhelming.

It seems we are at a standoff. If Harry goes to the ball game, he will feel uncomfortable because he did not leave Mary comfortably at home. His conscience will bother him. If Harry does not go to the ball game, he will feel resentful of the limitations Mary's problem is placing upon him.

Mary, on the other hand, feels guilty about asking Harry not to go to the game. She also feels ashamed that she had to beg him not to go. Now we have two people dealing with anger, guilt, confusion, resentment and many other emotions because of their interpretation of what is really taking place.

If Harry accepted that Mary's fears were real and rational to her, he could have thought of some workable options that would allow him to go to the ball game without guilt. All he had to do was think, "What would make Mary feel secure while I am gone?"

Possible options are:

1. Have a friend, neighbor, relative or other trusted person stay with Mary while he was gone. He would not have to go into details about Mary's condition, which I am sure she is trying to hide from the world. He could simply say Mary wasn't feeling well and does not want to be alone. Anyone could relate to that type of situation and would respond in a positive manner.

2. Harry could prepare for these contingencies by getting a pocket pager. This is also known as a beeper. Many doctors and other professionals use them so that they can be contacted when away from the office. In the same way, Harry could be contacted when he is away from home. Mary's knowing that she could contact Harry would eliminate most of the negative fear. The cost of less than $20.00 per month could have an emotional return that would far exceed it.

Let us explore some of the more common fears of agoraphobics and explain their causes:

Fears Created by the Feelings of Being Trapped or Feelings of Commitment

Driving alone

Taking a bath or shower with no one in the house

Writing a check or signing a document in public

Being in church, a restaurant, a theater, a shopping mall or any other public place

Going shopping alone

Taking a walk alone

Uninvited guests dropping in

Going to a party or family function

Going to a wedding or funeral

Going to a strangers house

Going on vacation to a strange city or location

Planes, buses, trains or any other public transportation

Beauty salons or barber shops

All of the above, and many more that could be added, are fearful to the agoraphobic because of the feelings of being trapped or feelings of commitment. The fantasy is always the same and the scenario is, "What if I panic in this situation? What will people think? I will make a fool of myself. My family will be embarrassed. I will not be able to leave without everyone being aware that there is something wrong. They will think I am crazy. It is too threatening. I will not, or cannot, go."

Fears Based on Reality, but Over-reacted To

Illness, either your own or others

Pregnancy

Upcoming events or situations that might be stressful

Anticipating surgery

Going to doctor

Going to dentist

Support person taking trip

Being left alone

Going on a trip

Going to a meeting (PTA, etc)

Upcoming holidays

All of the above, plus many others that could be added are based on events that enter all of our lives at one time or another. In other words, they are the reality of living. Many people who are non-agoraphobic react to these events or situations with some nervous anticipation. The agoraphobic, however, not only reacts, but over-reacts, creating more anxiety than is warranted.

Although fear is a natural and normal emotion, it is difficult to overcome when the emotion reaches high levels. The trick is to deal with the fear as soon as the thought process starts. If you allow yourself to ponder the fearful situation or event, the fantasy or scenario becomes more and more real to the subconscious mind. Some of the techniques that can be used have been discussed in previous chapters.

Others that I find more specifically designed to be used for overcoming fearful thoughts are:

Becoming Pre-programmed to Automatically Reduce the Levels of Anxiety

This is a technique used very successfully at the New Beginning Foundation. The agoraphobic is programmed on a subconscious level to respond to a simple hand signal to automatically breath slowly, externalize and feel calm and controlled when feelings of anticipatory fear enter their thoughts. Self-hypnotic techniques are used in this process.

Giving Yourself Affirmations to Overcome the Fear

Saying aloud or to yourself, "This is not acceptable" or "I am calm. I am in control" over and over again can reduce the fear.

Self Imagery

Visualizing yourself in a safe and secure place or situation will alleviate the feelings of fear.

Conscious Knowledge of Your Reactions

Become aware if you are over-reacting to a situation or event that calls for an anxious reaction. In other words, you are allowed to react, but a over-reaction is not called for. You can handle the normal reaction without over-reacting.

"I Don't Give a Damn" Attitude

Develop an attitude that no matter what happens, you are going to face it. This is not as tough as it seems. Combine the feeling of "I don't give a damn" with a feeling of anger about your limitations. You will be amazed at how well this technique works.

Nurturing Parent Speaking to Fearful Child

I have discussed previously that we all have a parent, child and adult within our emotional personalities. We can use each of these in an appropriate manner to control the other personalities. When the child within you is creating fear, assume the role of *nurturing* parent and have a mental conversation with that child. Tell him or her that it is going to be alright and that you (the nurturing parent) will take care of him or her. If you can, visualize the child and yourself as parent having the conversation. This is a very powerful technique.

Realize That You Have Options Available to You

One of the traits of the agoraphobic personality is the non-realization of options and alternatives. We paint ourselves into corners constantly. You always have ways of getting out of corners, if you allow yourself to be sensible and creative. For instance, if you are in line at the Post Office and the line is long and moving slowly, allow yourself to leave and come back another time, perhaps early in the morning, when the line is shorter. You do not have to stay there and feel fear, anxiety and stress. No "normal" person feeling that way would stay and suffer. Why should you? Always consider what options you have open to you.

Develop a Sense of Faith in Yourself

You have faced many stressful situations and even felt very anxious and survived. Anxiety will not kill you. Have faith that you can handle whatever comes up, no matter what you feel or experience.

The "Flowing Through" Technique

When feeling fearful, do not fight the feeling. Sit quietly, breathing slowly and deeply, and allow the feeling to grow. Be patient. It will soon peak and then reduce in its level of intensity. Think calming thoughts while this is going on. Assure yourself that this will soon pass. When it has leveled off and has reached acceptable levels, resume what you were doing while continuing to breath slowly and calmly. This technique becomes stronger with practice.

Avoidance

If you must avoid a fearful situation or event, give yourself permission to do so without guilt or remorse. Instead of saying "I couldn't do it," say "I chose not to do it." Realize it is your choice to do or not do anything in your life.

Taking Risk

There is no question that in order to recover from agoraphobia you are going to have take risks. This is the only way to grow, both in confidence and in emotional maturity. Risk taking is fearful to everyone, not just agoraphobics. There is always the fear of the unknown.

I am not in favor of taking risks to test or challenge yourself. I feel that the anxiety that this type of risk taking invokes overcomes any possibility of a true success in accomplishing the goal. You have to properly prepare for risk taking. You would not jump into a pool without the basic knowledge of how to swim. Why would you venture forth into a risky situation without the knowledge of how to handle contingencies that situation might create?

Much of this book deals with techniques on risk taking. Attitudes of confidence, techniques of anxiety control, self psyching, faith in yourself . . . all have to be involved in risk taking.

Taking risks call for motivation. You take the risk because *you* want or need to, not because someone else says you should or have to. You do not have to create risks. Life will take care of that for you. Things will come into your life to challenge you.

If you are properly prepared, you will have true successes when you take a risk. You will feel pleased about how you handled it. You will know inside that you have had an accomplishment that is bringing you further along your road to recovery.

If you find yourself at a stand still and risks are not coming into your life, be patient. They will come when you are ready for them.

Practice is important. This differs from challenging yourself. When you challenge yourself, you are setting yourself up for passing or failing. This does not apply to practice. There is no passing or failing. You can do it or not do it. Both are OK. You can drive one block or one mile. Either is OK. You can sit in front of a store or go in. Either way is alright. If you feel that you would like to walk into the store and then leave, that's OK too.

Remember, you are just practicing. With enough practice, you will be more comfortable with these things and will allow yourself to go further, when you are ready. Use all of your support systems when you are practicing. Remember, the goal is to have a true success, one where you felt comfortable taking the risk.

The following was sent to me by a recovered agoraphobic. It was written by Dr. David Viscott. To me, it says it all:

To laugh is to risk appearing the fool.
　　To weep is to risk appearing sentimental.
To reach out for another is to risk involvement.
To expose feelings is to risk exposing your true self
To place your ideas, your dreams, before the crowd is to risk their loss.
To love is to risk not being loved in return
To live is to risk dying
To hope is to risk despair.
To try is to risk failure.
But, risk must be taken, because the greatest hazard in life is to risk nothing.
The person who risks nothing, does nothing, has nothing, and is nothing.
He may avoid suffering and sorrow, but he simply cannot learn, feel, change, grow, love, live.
Chained by his certitudes, he is a slave, he has forfeited freedom.
ONLY A PERSON WHO RISKS . . . IS FREE!!!!

Anger 10

Agoraphobics, because of their need to control their emotions, are fearful of showing anger. The imagined scenario is "If I really get angry . . . if I really let it all out . . . I could kill someone." The anger has been suppressed for so many years that it could be compared to a latent volcano that could suddenly become active and wreak havoc upon all who may be around at that time.

This fear of releasing the angry feelings is so strong that the agoraphobic usually will not allow anger to be shown even under the most stressful situations. Of course there are exceptions. However, even at those times, the real intensity of the anger is suppressed and the true feelings are not shown. The agoraphobic wife might get angry at her husband, but it is usually shown to him as frustration rather than anger. She is fearful of letting her true feelings be known.

Suppressing any emotion is unhealthy . . . particularly an emotion as strong as anger. When it is held in, it festers. The person who does not release the feeling is a walking steam kettle with the opening sealed. The pressure builds and builds and demands to be released. If the anger is denied, it is released in other ways, such as in periods of crying, depression, fatigue, lethargy or withdrawal. We resist releasing the anger for fear of what may happen if we do so.

I can remember two instances in which I allowed my feelings of anger to be fully released. Both times I was so provoked that I could not suppress the feelings any longer. To my surprise, the results were not what I expected. I did not become hysterical, babbling like a fool and lashing out. I did shout and yell, but I said what had to be said. When it all came out, a feeling of peace came over me such as I had never experienced before. It was as though I was purged. A tremendous weight was lifted from my body. It felt good.

The reaction to my anger was not what I expected. The person I was angry at did not attack me. Instead he backed off and apologized. It was nothing like I fantasized. I have since learned to look at anger as an emotion which can be handled in many ways, not just in the fantasy of violent release and being destructive.

In the life of the agoraphobic, there are many situations which can create feelings of anger. She can be angry at herself as well as others. She can be angry at the unfairness of being a limited person. She can be angry at her family and friends for not understanding her problems. She can be angry at the predicaments others can put her in because of their lack of understanding. She can be angry at making a mistake. She can be angry at the weather. She can be angry at her parents. She can be angry for lack of support when needed. We can go on and on.

Anger does not have to make sense . . . it is an emotion and emotions are not always logical. They just are. They are neither right or wrong, good or bad. It is what we do with them, or our response to the emotion, that is important. We learn in our childhood years how to respond to anger. If our parents stifle any display of anger from the child, we learn to suppress the feeling. It in not uncommon for the child to be punished if anger is shown, especially against the parental figure. It can be easily understood, then, why the adult will not show anger. The subconscious thought is punishment will follow.

In many cases parents are dealing with their own problems and are themselves angry persons. That anger can be shown by being physically or verbally abusive towards the child. In my case, verbal abuse was the norm. I remember thinking "I wish she would hit me rather than yell at me." To this day, I cringe inside when I see a mother yelling at a child.

Many people, especially agoraphobics, will not show anger because of the fear of losing another's love, or sometimes even more important, support. It is easier for a non-agoraphobic to take that risk than it is for an agoraphobic. The agoraphobic support system is needed for survival. The threat of being left without support, such as being left alone, will prevent showing anger, or even displeasure with another.

Since we are constantly seeking the love and approval of others, we hold in the anger. This suppression creates another feeling . . . frustration. We want to say things and cannot. We want to vent our feelings, but are prevented from doing so by the "What if's." The fantasy is, "If the other person does not like me, they will not be there to help me, if needed. I cannot take that risk." And so, we become people pleasers, playing the game of straddling the fence, not making waves and generally being "so good." If the world only knew what was going on inside of us.

In order to grow out of agoraphobia, we must learn coping techniques in handling the anger constructively, not destructively. Much has been written on the subject, but very little with the agoraphobic personality in mind. We must handle our anger a little differently than the "civilian" world. While we are dependent on others, we have to be careful how and to whom we release the anger. We must realize certain approaches to releasing anger can have good results and others can have bad results. This has to be our first judgement . . . What are the consequences if we let go?

If we are angry with a person who is not critically important in our lives, we can approach that person and tell him of our feelings of anger. We are not actually threatened if that person does not love us, even though we want to be loved by one and all. We must discern. How you let that person know your anger should be thought out in advance. You have choices. You can calmly explain your feelings about what was said or done to make you angry. Or you can let it all out and scream and yell. It all depends on how you want to get the message across. Remember, this person is not important in your life or support system. It is not wise to become physical in order to release anger. You are a mature individual, not a spoiled brat. Act as one.

In the case of showing anger against someone who is important to you, the approach is different. You have to maintain a level of dignity and maturity and above all, avoid having that person become defensive. When you accuse someone, the natural instinct is for that person to defend his actions, thereby becoming defensive. Consider how you and your partner handle conflict. Does it go something like this?

- You confront your partner with an issue
- Your partner defends and counters
- You restate the issue with greater intensity, magnifying it beyond its original scope
- Your partner again defends and counters, this time possibly with a personal attack
- You defend against the personal attack and counter with a stronger personal attack. . . .

The battle escalates with each of you pelting the other with verbal and emotional bombs you hope will wear the other down to defeat. The real problem in this typical style of conflict resolution is that no one wins; everyone loses and the only thing that is accomplished is feelings of frustration and more anger.

In sharing anger, the goal is not only to release the anger, but to seek solutions so that the circumstances which created the anger are not repeated. Seek solutions, not necessarily victory over the other person. Realize that the anger exists and has to be resolved and that it is a problem between the two of you, not just yours or his. Think of the anger as the enemy . . . not your partner. In doing this, you and your partner work towards resolving the anger, not fixing blame. Realize that much of the anger is based on childlike reactions to a circumstance and may be an overreaction.

Instead of starting the discussion with "You did this or that and you hurt me", describe your feelings, such as, "When you did this or that, I *felt* hurt." The difference is bringing the discussion down to a feeling level, which is where the anger exists.

Share your feelings in a loving way, not by accusing, but by explaining why you felt hurt.

Acknowledge that you know the hurt was not intentional and that your partner was probably not aware that you felt hurt. Inflicting hurt upon another is usually unintentional. If you feel it was intentional, then you have to go deeper and identify the real problem. It could be frustration, resentment or lack of feelings of respect and consideration.

Above all, remain calm and considerate of the others feelings and responses. You have told him how you felt, now you are seeking solutions. That is the goal.

Allow you partner to share his feelings and listen with understanding and consideration. All situations of this sort have two sides to the story. Until both sides are known, solutions cannot be reached.

If you have both agreed that hurt was caused which created anger, brainstorm solutions so that the act will not be repeated.

It is best to write down all possible solutions whether they are realistic or not. Input is needed from both parties.

When the list is complete, and only then, go back through it and eliminate solutions that are unacceptable to one or both of you. After you have completed this brain-storming session, you should be left with a few acceptable solutions to the problem that you both can live with.

Vow to be aware of the other's feelings in the future and not to repeat the situation that created the anger.

In practicing this approach to dealing with anger or other conflicts, you can get away from the "victory at all costs" syndrome and its unhappy consequences, and become better at identifying and defeating a common enemy while strengthening your relationship.

There are times when the person you wish to vent your anger against may have died and you still harbor feelings of anger against him. Or, it may be a person that is too threatening to let him know of your anger. This is a technique that can be used effectively to release the anger.

Write a letter to that person sharing all of your feelings of anger and the reasons for those feelings. *THIS LETTER IS FOR YOUR EYES ONLY AND IS NOT TO BE MAILED OR TO BE DISCUSSED WITH ANYONE ELSE.* Use foul language, if that is what you feel. Let it all out. Be very explicit. Then, put the letter away for two days. Take it out again and re-read it. Make changes, if necessary. If you are satisfied that the letter says exactly what you want it to say, do the following:

Place two chairs across from each other, facing each other.

Sit in one chair and read the letter out loud to the other chair which symbolizes the person the letter is directed to.

Read the letter with feeling and allow your emotions to be released. Cry, shout, scream . . . it's all acceptable. You are releasing the anger . . . the pent up steam that has been creating your frustration.

When you are finished, burn the letter and go on with your life.

Considering the lifestyle of an active agoraphobic, a certain amount of anger is justified and should be acknowledged as such. It would be unrealistic to think that he or she has no cause for anger. The constant anxiety, the limitations, the non-understanding, the lack of consideration of others, the constant negative anticipation . . . all of these and many other causes for anger are justified. The worst thing you can do is to deny the feelings of anger about these circumstances. Discuss and share these feelings with someone you trust, not to reach solutions, but to vent the feelings. The solution is to work towards recovery from agoraphobia. As you go down the path towards recovery, much of the anger will disappear or minimize in importance.

Anger can be used as a motivator. If we are angry enough about not being able to deal with a situation or event, it might motivate us to use the "I don't give a damn" approach discussed in the chapter entitled "Fear and Risk." It is impossible to feel two emotions at the same time. Anger can overcome anxiety. It can be a positive force instead of a negative one.

Self confidence and self esteem are integral parts of your feelings when facing anger. The insecurity of possibly losing love, the feelings of inadequacy in sharing your emotions, the attitudes of "I should not (do not deserve to) feel this way," all repress your ability to show anger. You will find that when your feelings of self worth increase, you will feel less threatened in revealing your true feelings.

Anger is a normal and necessary emotion. Denying the feeling can cause long lasting damage, both psychological and physical, so deal with it in a constructive manner.

Manage it effectively and efficiently as soon as you can after a situation or event that causes anger. Do not let it fester.

Have the courage to share your feelings. It is a necessary risk.

Have faith that others that will acknowledge and respond to your feelings. If they do not, and you feel let down, use the letter technique described in this chapter.

One way or another, release your anger . . . .

And then go forward *TOWARDS YOUR RECOVERY!!!*

The Fearful Child   11

As Founding Director of the New Beginning Foundation, I lecture at "Open Forums on Agoraphobia." During the lecture I describe the child's belief system of feeling emotionally fearful, insecure and inadequate. Afterwards, many parents will approach me and share their concern about the possibility of their children being agoraphobic.

They tell me of instances of fear, shyness, insecurity, irrational behavior, waking during the night, sleepwalking, bed wetting and other behaviors and ask "Does this mean my child will be an agoraphobic?"

An agoraphobic parent is especially concerned about their child's emotional stability and may have feelings of guilt about their being agoraphobic and how that might affect their children's future.

I have been asked about genetic carry-overs in agoraphobic families. Many agoraphobics have had an agoraphobic parent and fear that the problem is inherited. To the best of my knowledge, there has not been any verified research in this area. There are cases of agoraphobic children coming from agoraphobic parents, but I feel that this may be due more to childhood input than to genetic programming. However, I must state that the possibility does exist and perhaps some future researcher might do an accurate study in this area. Whether it exists or not should not be a major concern, since I have found that those agoraphobics I have worked with that come from an agoraphobic parent recover as well as those that do not.

I do not know of any accurate way of determining whether or not a child will grow into an agoraphobic. Many fears are outgrown by the child as their emotional belief system is developing. As they experience more and more people, activities, situations and events, they may change in their attitudes and eliminate "childish" fears and reactions. They may grow emotionally into "normal" adults.

Many fears a young child exhibits are perfectly normal since they are instinctive. This could include the fear of heights or the fear of falling. Other fears could stem from upsetting experiences such as a near accident or a threatening situation.

Fear of strangers is usually prevalent in children of about 8 months old. The child may cry when a stranger approaches. This could be a baby sitter or a relative they do not see often. However, these fears usually disappear by the age of two or three.

As a child becomes aware of his natural environment, he may become fearful of lightning, darkness or thunder storms. These fears are usually outgrown as the child realizes that his environment is safe and that these phenomena are normal.

Fears of monsters, spiders and dark corners are not unusual in three or four year olds. Input from television and "scary stories" affect them. Again, these fears are usually outgrown.

The most common "phobia" among children from the age of six through adolescence is a fear of school, or "school phobia." Many children will manifest this fear into physical symptoms such as headaches and nausea at the start of the day to avoid going to school. Some school related anxiety is normal. However, when it affects the child physically and it is prolonged, it should be investigated. If the child is determined to be a true "school phobic," psychological counselling should be used to help the child through this problem. Parental support and understanding must be included in the help the child receives.

The world is full of things that any right-minded child would and should be afraid of. Some dogs are vicious and should be feared and avoided. Some strangers could harm the child. Being outdoors during a lightening storm could be a dangerous thing to do. The child should be encouraged to recognize this type of fear as rational and these fears should not be extinguished. They should be taught appropriate rules of action when faced with these rational fears.

The advent of television has brought the world's suffering into the child's life. Yes, it could be a fearful world, especially when you are not prepared by experience to distinguish between what might and might not affect you directly. It is not surprising that children have bad dreams or nightmares after a particularly scary television program or movie. Discretion must be used by the parent, and, if the child is particularly sensitive to certain television programs or movies, these should be avoided until the child is emotionally secure enough to deal with them.

Separation from the parent, particularly the mother, can create fear in a child. In such relationships, the mother is usually overindulgent or extremely severe, controlling the child's emotions. Sometimes the child is worried about a parent who is ill, and is fearful of leaving home. In some instances, the child who was left alone or with a "stranger" (baby sitter) before he felt ready will form an overdependency to be with the parent. Separation from the child before he or she is ready can create many future problems and should be avoided.

The "fearful" parent can convey many messages to the child that becomes the child's belief system. Messages such as "Don't cross the street. You *will* get hit by a car" or "Don't climb the tree. You *will* fall and break your arm." can affect the child. The real message the child hears is "Don't take risks. If you do, they will have catastrophic results." Risk taking is necessary for growth. The "fearful" parent stifles that growth by conveying these messages to the child. In many instances, it is the parent's fear that creates the non-risk taking, fearful child. This does not mean you avoid all advice on taking risks. It means you discern between what is a necessary risk for growth and exploration and what is actually a risk that can cause harm and danger.

Childhood fears could fall between being rational and irrational. Fear of the dark may be picked up from stories, fairy tales and horror movies. To the sensitive child, many bad things can happen in the dark. This may be thought of as an irrational fear. However, the loss of light that accompanies darkness results in a loss of familiar points of reference that give stability and order to the child's surroundings. So, it can also be thought of as rational. It is important for the parent to discern the difference and take necessary steps to deal with the child's fear. A simple night light could help avoid future problems.

Fears of injury, illness or other handicaps are a bit more difficult to respond to because we cannot guarantee to the child that they will never become sick or disabled. Sometimes this fear stems from the child's belief that his or her own "evil" behavior will be punished by injury. If you suspect this is the case, the child must be assured that illness or accidents are not caused by misbehavior and explanations should be given of the true causes of disease and injury. If the behavior persists, psychological counseling is called for.

Sometimes, children fear their own fears. They become anxious and apprehensive in anticipation of becoming overcome by fear. The child feels afraid that they will become afraid in some new or unfamiliar situation or event. This is not the same "fear of fear" that the agoraphobic experiences. It is very common amongst children to have this fear and the child should be assured that this fear is "normal" and will pass as they become more secure in the world around them.

Children CAN become depressed, although the signs of depression in children differ from those of adults. Unfortunately, there is no simple check list to determine whether a child is truly depressed. Some children appear sad, lost, or lack a zest for life, but that does not necessarily mean they are depressed. They may be tired, under-nourished, concerned about some up-coming event, or have a physical problem. These avenues should be explored by the parent before determining whether the child is truly depressed. Children do not have the ability to deal with some realities of life as adults do. The loss of a relative, friend, or even a pet, can create depression in the child. They may appear to recover quickly, but may react to the loss repeatedly during their early life. Usually the child's feelings of depression will pass. If they do not, further investigation should be made and appropriate steps taken.

I have previously stated that the agoraphobic personality is developed in early childhood by negative input from the parents. If you are concerned about your child's emotional stability during their adult life, some of the following hints may be of use to you. Apply them in your child's life now, and a "normal," functional adult will be your reward.

Let Your Child Grow at His or Her Own Rate

Do not make the mistake of comparing your child with other children his own age. Growth is very individual and forcing a child to perform acts he is not ready for can be very damaging. It is helpful to know typical progression rates and learning levels, but remember, these are just guides. Let your child grow at his/her own rate and you will protect self-esteem.

Cuddle and Caress Your Child

Studies have indicated that children who are held, caressed, cuddled and nurtured have a higher level of self esteem. The child who is given a lot of affection makes much more rapid progress than the child who isn't. The child who is cuddled feels more secure and important. Show your child you care by cuddling and caressing him or her often.

Teach the Child His or Her Importance as Part of the Family

We are all social animals and have a need to belong to a group. This need is especially prevalent in the child. A secure family environment increases the child's sense of belonging. Include the child, no matter how young, in family get-togethers and events. If the opportunity arises, and the child is ready, include him or her in future family planning. Listen to his input. You may be surprised what knowledge you may gain of your child's thinking and attitude processes.

Let the Child Be an Individual and Unique

Avoid comparisons. When you start comparing your children with one another, two things will happen. One is that improvement *does not* come and the second is that the child who is on the negative end of the comparison will lose self esteem. The message the child hears is "However much I may love you, I love your brother/sister/cousin/friend more. They are much more worthy of my love." That's a heavy burden for a child to carry. It makes the parents love conditional. The condition is "Be like someone else, and then, I will love you." Avoid doing this to your child at all costs. It could be very damaging for future growth and relationships.

Compliment the Child

We all need "strokes," especially children. Look for the good, even in situations that might seem disastrous at the time. If a child helps with the dishes and breaks one, do not criticize for the broken dish, but compliment for the desire to help. In looking for the good in the child, you will build her self-esteem. You help her see that she has worth, and even though she is not perfect, she is loved.

Give Your Child Time with You

Many parents are so involved in their own lives, that they do not find time to share with their children. They are missing out on a great joy. Children can be invigorating and challenging. However, you must "set the stage" for your time spent with them. You should give them the "right kind of time." Children's need differ. They might need quiet time before bed and a reading of a story may be appropriate. They may need play time and some playful wrestling may be in order. Just sitting quietly and watching television together can be very reassuring to a child. Quantity time does not substitute for quality time. Plan your time together for both your benefits.

Teach Your Child Honesty

Children are not born with the ability to lie. They learn to do so out of fear. Lying decreases the child's self esteem. If you are totally honest with your child, he will learn that lying is not necessary or acceptable. Let the child know that punishment will not follow honesty, no matter what the problem was. Create a climate for honesty. Never open the door for a lie. If the child broke a bowl, do not ask "Who did this?" Instead, say "I noticed you broke the bowl", and then have it out. When you suspect he or she is lying, tell him so . . . kindly. Tell him that it might seem safer and easier to tell a lie, but he will feel much better about himself if he tells the truth. You are the living example in your child's life. If you are honest with him or her, your child will be honest with you.

Let Your Child Grow Creatively

Every child has inborn creativity. Encourage it. When you do so, you will increase his/her self esteem. You let your child know that he/she is an individual and has worth. Stifling creativity in the early years can create an adult who will be afraid to think, do or fend for himself.

Teach Your Child Fairness

Children do not inherently know what is fair or unfair. They must be taught. If your son plays with his sister's toy, he will not know it is unfair not to share or return it to her, since it is hers. Using the approach that the child is selfish if he doesn't share is not the way to teach fairness. Rather, explain to the child that the toy is to be shared with his sister and that it is her toy. Let the child know the value of personal possessions early in life and to respect that. Reverse the situation and ask the child if his sister can play with one of his toys while he play with hers. Fairness is a necessary trait in dealing with life as an adult.

Teach Your Child to Be Persevering

A child with high self esteem and confidence is usually one that is persevering. She will follow through on a task, whether it is a jigsaw puzzle or a school assignment. Encourage your child to persevere. This does not mean "force" him or her to have persistence. Encouragement means just that. A message such as "I'm glad that you're working so well on that puzzle. I know it's hard for you, but I'm glad you're not giving up. Keep it up." can go a long way in creating a higher level of self esteem.

Do Not Always Rescue Your Child. Let Him Make Mistakes

Contrary to popular belief, we do not learn from our successes. We learn from our mistakes. The child cannot grow unless mistakes are made, and then, corrected. He or she will learn how to handle the negatives of life by experiencing those negatives and learning to make adjustments. If a child bumps his head under a table enough times, he will learn not to stand up under a table. If you rescue him the first time he bumps his head, all he will learn is that you will be there if he gets into trouble. Many adults deal with life this way, always needing rescuing. Don't let this happen to your child. Let him make mistakes . . . and learn.

Our childhood experiences determine what kind of adults we will be. If you are fearful for your child, be you agoraphobic or not, practice these rules during your children's formative years, and I assure you, agoraphobia will not enter their lives.

If you are an agoraphobic, the most positive thing you can do for your child is to do everything possible to recover. Your example of dealing with the problem will be an inspiration for your child that will stay with him the rest of his life. Many agoraphobics hide their condition from their children. You are only fooling yourself. They know you are not like other parents. If your child is old enough, let them read this book. He wants to understand you. With understanding comes love. Your child can be your strongest motivation to get through this problem. He wants to help. Let him!

The Female Agoraphobic

12

Statistically there are more female agoraphobics than male. The percentages vary from as high as 90% to as low as 60% according to what you read and what the source is. No matter what the source, the female agoraphobic dominates the statistics.

The main reason for this high percentage is a sociological one. Agoraphobic limitations creates a dependent, passive individual. In our society, it is more acceptable for the female to assume that role. We have all heard statements such as "My little wife . . . she never wants to go anywhere. All she wants to do is stay at home. But, she's a great cook and homemaker and takes care of the kids. Besides, she's a little nervous and shy." And people remark "What a good wife she is . . . how dedicated to the family. Isn't that wonderful."

Equal rights aside, familiar sayings, such as "A woman's place is in the home" reinforces the acceptance of a woman being a shy, passive and compliant person. Often, when a woman goes to her doctor and complains of nervousness, the doctor smiles indulgently and tells her she is under a little stress and not to worry about it. He may give her a mild tranquilizer and sends her home. After all, she is a woman and women get nervous easily. He may not take her seriously. She's not a man. She doesn't have to face the world like he does. She doesn't face the stress a man does.

If she does not respond to the medication, the doctor may look for other causes, such as her menstrual cycle or perhaps she is menopausal. She tries to tell him that these feelings are different, but again, she is not taken seriously. She is sent home, frustrated and confused. She knows there is something seriously wrong. She is feeling fearful and anxious and most of all, frustrated. She knows she is not being taken seriously by her doctor, and her husband is reacting the same way. After all, she is only a woman . . . and women are prone to be nervous.

As time passes, her fear and anxiety grow. She may have even experienced a panic attack. However, her obvious concern and discomfort are ignored or played down. It is not until the symptoms continue over long period of time and her household starts to become affected, that someone suggests she see a mental health professional. Because of her confusion and lack of information, she does not know what to say to the doctor. She tells him of vague feelings and he explores her background and current family life. She tells him of her "nervousness" and he prescribes more medication. She tells him of her fear of going crazy, and he tells her that is why she is there. She leaves, again, with a feeling of "no one understands." She knows she is not being taken seriously. She is looked at as just another "nervous" woman.

Eventually, she gives up. She comes to the conclusion that she is crazy, and no one can help her. She does less and less outside her home. Her husband assumes most of the shopping and outside errands. She finds herself crying for no apparent reason. She is constantly anxious, but fights the feelings. Friends are starting to ignore her because she will not participate in social functions. Advice from family members who are concerned is ignored. They do not understand either. The children are confused because Mom no longer is available for PTA meetings and other school functions. Over a period of time, those around her start to believe she is "weird" and must have a mental condition.

Her husband starts to become irritated with the situation, thinking thoughts like "she is doing this to get attention" or "it's her menopause" and he starts to ignore her pleas for help and understanding. She finds herself all alone and miserable in a home that once gave her pleasure. Her self esteem and sense of worth diminish to the point of thinking of herself as a totally useless person.

She may start drinking, finding alcohol relieves the fearful feelings. It may even make her feel "almost normal" and she finds she can go to some places if she has a couple of drinks first. Her husband encourages this, since the pressure is being taken off of him. He cannot conceive that his wife may be turning into an alcoholic. Neither can she, but she becomes aware that more and more alcohol is needed to allow her to be functional. When she is not drinking, the old feelings return, magnified by the results of alcoholic hangovers. So, she drinks more. Since drinking is socially acceptable, again her obvious cry for help is ignored. She is a woman, and therefore, she is weak.

It is not until she starts having blackouts and other results of her drinking that any concern is shown. By then, she is dependent on the liquor and refuses to give it up. It is the only thing she has that can give her some feelings of normalcy. Now she is thought of as a "crazy" person and also an alcoholic. Still, her cries for help and understanding are ignored.

As time passes, and she becomes more and more limited, she may become home bound. She finds it very difficult to do her housework, and the home she once had great pride in starts to show the affects of her non-involvement. She may cook fewer meals and spend her days watching television or reading. Her family is becoming more concerned, not because of her suffering, but because the chores she used to handle are not being done.

Conversely, she may let her perfectionist personality dominate her. She becomes obsessive about her house-work. She may become angry at a dirty ashtray, cleaning it over and over again. She may vacuum three times a day. She may feel if her house is in order, so is her life.

Many conflicts arise and resentment abounds. "What are we going to do about her" they ask. They take her through another round with the doctors, and she becomes more depressed. After a while, she becomes a non-person in her own home. Things are being done around her, not with her. Concern is shown only when she is obviously suffering, and even then, she knows she is only being tolerated, not understood.

During all of this time, she has not been taken seriously by her family or the professionals she has seen. After all, she is only a woman. The family is falling apart. Her husband is angry and frustrated. Her children ignore her. She is convinced she is "crazy". . . and all of this could have been prevented with proper diagnosis at the beginning of her problem. What a waste.

I would like to share a letter with you that was sent to me by a woman in Canada. In many ways it tells the story better than I can.

CASE HISTORY—"D.V."

Dear Mr. Green:

I have been wanting to write to you for a very long time. I have received the information on your Foundation and was very impressed by what it said. I have shown it to my parents and my ex-husband, but they just laughed and said that they would put me in a mental institution if I told anyone I have agoraphobia.

I have been to many doctors and psychiatrists, some who have never heard of agoraphobia and others that have no idea how to treat it. Right now I'm so confused and tired of hoping for someone to help me. I can't give up because I know there is such a beautiful world out there to enjoy.

My husband left me after three years of having this problem. At first he said he understood, but as time passed he started to get angry at me and yelled a lot. My daughter went to live with my parents, so I am all alone. I couldn't leave my home and made excuses to my friends not to see them. I didn't even want them to come here, because I was afraid they would ask a lot of questions.

I get nerve pills from my doctor, but they do not seem to help much. I have started to drink and that helps, but I am frightened that I will become an alcoholic. I hardly go out because I get so frightened. I have gained a lot of weight and feel disgusted when I see myself in the mirror.

No one seems to care anymore and I feel all alone. I cry a lot, but it doesn't help. I have spoken to my Pastor, and he gives me spiritual counselling. But, I need more.

Now my life has become even more disgusting. I rent a house and I rent out the basement apartment. Eventually I confided my situation to the old man that rents the apartment. He is 63 years old, fat, cranky and a despicable person. As you can tell I can't stand the sight of him now.

I guess he saw a golden opportunity to help himself out. Before I told him, he at least took me to buy groceries, pay bills, etc. After finding that I had this problem, he threatened to leave unless I had sex with him. A year later he is still here and insists on sex every morning. From the start it made me so sick, afterwards I'd run to the bathroom and throw up. But he has managed to get me totally dependent on him and I hate myself for that. I drink a lot when I think about it. He seems to have full control over me. I don't go anywhere unless it's with him, and I'm only 36. I want to be with people my own age so bad, I can't sleep at night anymore. I just lay and cry and I'm becoming so depressed it scares me. I can't tell anyone about this, I am so ashamed. I don't know what to do.

My parent's are coming here from Toronto at Christmas time for my sister's wedding. I just don't know how I'm going to avoid the wedding. But I know I can't go. How can I go on avoiding life forever?

I feel like my whole life stopped three years ago. I used to be so happy and loved living life. I had good friends and family, and now, nothing. I can't even remember the last time I laughed. I have thought of suicide, but I cannot do that to my daughter. Besides, I don't want to die, but I sure would like to live.

I keep looking for help, but I can't go to any more doctors. I don't have the money, and anyway, they don't seem to understand. They have told me it would pass, I'm just going through a phase and they give me pills. I read whatever I can, but I don't understand how this could happen to me.

Please help me out of this nightmare.

Thank you.
D.V.

"D" joined our program approximately a year ago and has turned her life around. Her levels of confidence and self esteem have grown tremendously and she is working. Her first act of independence was to throw the old man out. All she needed was to use the courage we all have to make the choice. Once that was done, she started to handle her own life and learned to take small risks. Small risks are leading her into larger challenges, which she is handling. I am very proud of her and know she will be a whole person once again.

Her letter describes a life that could have continued down a destructive path. No one cared and she was ignored by those who were closest to her. It may sound over-dramatic, but we know this is not so. Even those agoraphobics that are still in a family environment are suffering from non-understanding spouses and family. They are also seeking answers and help.

The female agoraphobic can easily become a victim of her own environment. Because of other people's lack of understanding and not taking her cries for help seriously, she can feel they are right and start to ignore or block her own intuitive feelings. This attitude can prevent her from seeking proper help and lead her down a path of doctor after doctor, all trying their best, but not dealing with the problem.

The sense of insecurity, stemming from childhood programing, makes the female agoraphobic believe that others are wiser and know what is good for her. Her life script is a series of "don'ts." She has been told "don't" think for yourself . . . "don't" feel important . . . "don't" question an authority figure . . . "don't" be assertive or aggressive . . . "don't" get angry . . . "'don't" talk back and a whole series of other "don'ts" that have affected her as an adult. She needs constant affirmation and approval from others. Is it any wonder that she feels she must be dependent on others for what she thinks and does?

There is truth to the statement about women's intuition. Your intuition will let you know when you find the therapist or program that will be able to help you. When you do, go for it and don't allow the negative input of other people dissuade you. You are in control of your life, present and future.

In her growth out of agoraphobia, the female agoraphobic must learn to change her life script. Her feelings of dependency will change to feelings of a sharing independence. Her feelings of insecurity will change to feelings of confidence. Her feelings of being limited will change to those of being unlimited, being able to do what she wants to do. It is not the "impossible dream". *It is achievable!*

The Male Agoraphobic **13**

The male agoraphobic reminds me of the platypus. Many have seen and described it, but its existence was denied by the scientific world for many years. When it was finally "discovered" to exist, they believed it to be a freak of nature.

Statistics indicate the vast majority of agoraphobics are female. Figures as high as 95% have been published. Contrast that with our records at the New Beginning Foundation where approximately 40% of our clients are male. Perhaps this is a result of my public appearances in which I relate my experiences as an agoraphobic. Men can identify with me and realize that they are suffering the same symptoms and lifestyle I did when I was actively agoraphobic. I strongly believe that there are many more males coping with agoraphobia than we will ever know.

The primary reason in not admitting to having the fearful feelings and suffering the symptoms is simply that it is not "manly" to be a "weak," dependent, passive person in our society. Limitations created by physical causes are more socially acceptable. Those created by "childlike" fears are not. The man is supposed to be strong, fearless, nonemotional, a good provider, and, independent.

Since agoraphobia is created in early childhood by the negative input of others, why is it so surprising that male children can be programed as well as female children? Our susceptibility at an early age is exactly the same. Our needs for love and affirmation is the same. Our sensitivity is the same. Why then, does it not follow that our adult responses to childhood programing would be the same?

The chain of events described in this book that leads the female agoraphobic from latent to active agoraphobia is also similar. The circumstances may differ, but the end result is an adult feeling the fears, insecurities and inadequacies of the child he used to be.

Reflecting on my childhood, I know that I was an agoraphobic child. I was a "mama's boy." I was the end result of my mother's fears and insecurities, transferred to me by example and words. If I had had a sister instead of brothers, perhaps she would have been the recipient of this input. I was the daughter my mother never had, and, as such, the one that was "protected" by being told the catastrophic results of risk taking. I was also my mother's "support person," accompanying her on shopping trips and on other outside activities.

It was during my research on agoraphobia that I realized my mother was agoraphobic. Her fears became mine. A child cannot judge what is right or wrong, good or bad. The example of the parent becomes the belief system of the child. I could not be left alone, did not risk as others my age did, stayed close to home, and, developed the agoraphobic personality which was going to affect me the rest of my life.

The male agoraphobic develops a different set of coping skills in dealing with life than the female. He tries to disguise his "childlike" feelings with socially acceptable techniques. Drinking is socially acceptable, so he drinks to reduce the inner anxiety. Three martini lunches and a cocktail at the end of the day are not thought of as unusual. Did you ever wonder why bars open at 6:00 in the morning? The people who drink before starting their day are not all alcoholics. Most alcoholics would have a bottle at home. The sunrise drinkers, predominately male, need to fortify themselves before facing the challenges of the day.

Or the agoraphobic man may turn to tranquilizers which are socially acceptable, claiming the pressures of his job are getting to him. He can easily receive a prescription for medication from his doctor with total understanding and sympathy.

Finally, his fears create the inevitable panic attack, and he rushes to the doctor. The doctor, knowing how stressful a "man's world" is, will treat him differently than he would a woman. After all, he is the "warrior" fighting the world and he must be treated so that he can continue to do so. He is the "bread winner" of the family, or is on the ladder to accomplish his career goals, and must be supported.

All of this creates serious conflicts in the male agoraphobic. As a male, he is not supposed to experience these feelings of fear and anxiety without some outside influence creating them. His role is that of Clint Eastwood, not a fearful child. Of course, he cannot discuss this with anyone. Not only would no one understand, they would surely think he is crazy. He must stifle the feelings and somehow go on.

The problem is, no matter how much he disguises his inner fears from the outside world, they exist. All of the alcohol, all of the pills, will not take away the inner fear. He begins to anticipate and fear the possibility of a heart attack or stroke and this now dominates his thinking. He limits his physical activities and remains at home as much as possible. His insecurities affect his working life. His wife is confused. His children cannot understand why daddy does not take them fishing or on camping trips. As time passes, he becomes as limited as any agoraphobic, male or female, and the cycle of seeking help begins.

The frustrations suffered by the male agoraphobic can be more severe than those of the female, because it is more socially acceptable for the woman to be limited by emotional feelings, but the man's role does not allow this. The lack of understanding is multiplied because of the strangeness of his behavior. Therapies are directed to dealing with the stresses of life rather than the inner stresses of living.

Since he is the support of his family, he is forced to continue working. His home life and family relationships are jeopardized. His wife or girlfriend becomes his support person (mommy) and she does not understand her role. This is not the way it is supposed to be. The man is supposed to support the passive, dependent woman.

The seriousness of this situation cannot be over emphasized. The man's ego, values and role in life are on the line.

I would like to share three letters with you that I have received from male agoraphobics:

CASE HISTORY—"J.B.F"

Dear Mr. Green:

I enjoyed your presentation on a local N.Y. radio station on the subject of agoraphobia.

I have been a "cripple" since 1968. My problems started with 3 panic attacks within an 18 month period. The first examinations said it was metabolic and no follow up was even done to find the reason I had the attacks.

The first one occurred at a friend's house explaining to him why I could no longer go to work with him. The reason was a fearful drive along an extremely busy highway and working in an unheated building.

The friend had gotten me the job and I was afraid of losing his friendship. I had a panic attack at his house that morning while telling him I had to quit.

The fear of the attacks prevented me from working and I went on welfare. Some time later, I had an attack while behind the wheel. This was fifteen years ago and I have not driven a car since.

For the past 6 months I go nowhere except to work. I do not come in contact with any people because I work outside. Aside from that, I am afraid to go anywhere for fear I will have a panic attack and die. The panic attacks are unbearable.

My wife is a registered nurse, and although she doesn't understand, she is trying to be supportive. I have been tied down to $100.00 a week jobs so long, she has to work to support our family.

At present I am 42 years old. 5'11" and 280 pounds. Quite obese, you might say. I have been told I have hypoglycemia. I follow my doctor's instructions and watch my diet, but the panic attacks still come.

Yes, I've thought of suicide from time to time, but fortunately being a Jehovah's Witness wouldn't allow that.

I've been to a psychologist and she stated I didn't live within my limitations. In other words, I have to recognize my limitations and not step out of bounds. I do not feel this is right. I am not physically limited. I want to live as a man, not a "cripple." I'm tired of living this way. I want to be normal.

Please help me.

J. B. F.

CASE HISTORY—"L.G.R."

The next letter moved me to tears:

To Whom It May Concern:

I am an agoraphobic. I saw an article in the "Dear Abby" column of the local paper in which another agoraphobic was asking for someone to help them. Abby referred her to your organization—thus the reason for my letter.

I am forty years old and at the present time am unable to leave the house. My best friend, who I have lived with some 15 years has been looking after me.

I believe that I have had this problem most of my life, but it started to take control of my life when I was 23 years old. That's when I had my first attack at my job. I was working in the bookkeeping department at a local factory at the time of this attack. I was rushed to the hospital because they thought it was a heart attack. After I got out of the hospital and returned to work, I was getting very uneasy about being there and left my job and started working at a local hospital.

I realized that something was happening to me and that I could not stay where I was. I felt that by working at the hospital I would feel safe and try to find out what was happening to me.

I worked on the day shift as a psychiatric aide for about a year before I asked to be put on the midnight shift. The uneasy feeling I was experiencing was getting worse, but it seemed to subside when I isolated myself on the night shift. I continued to work on that shift for the next 8 years, but during that time I had stopped all social activities and only left the house to go to work.

The uneasy feeling had by now become a powerful fear and I was unable to leave the house alone and was forced to resign my job in October, 1978.

My friend, who had been looking after me through all this, started taking me to a psychiatrist and had to stay with me during my appointments. After seeing several psychiatrists, I started therapy with Dr. ----- and spent the next four years under his care—with little improvement.

Dr. ----- moved out of the area in June of last year and I am not in therapy at this time. I felt I would have to accept my condition and that it would not change. I had given up when Dr. ----- moved.

Last fall my friend was told he had cancer. Knowing that I could not survive without him, I became very depressed. I didn't know what I was going to do. I finally came to the conclusion that I would kill myself when he died. I have lived with that idea for the past 6 months.

I don't want to die. I want to live a normal life. I realize that it will take time to get over this. I don't want to give up and die.

I want to live.

L. G. R.

CASE HISTORY—"G.H."

The following letter describes more fully the feelings of frustration shared by male agoraphobics:

To The New Beginning Foundation:

I saw one of your representatives on TV and I hope you can help me.

I am 26 years old and married. Our income is tightly budgeted, otherwise I'd have looked for help long ago. My wife listens, but I'm sure she doesn't understand. Sometimes I almost wish it would happen to her just once so she could see what I am going through. I love her very much, but I can't be the husband I want to be because of this sick thing I am carrying around with me.

My life is very limited. I can't go to a lot of places in my own neighborhood even though I've lived here all my life. I can't even go for a job. I always get too panicky to go to the interview. I'm losing all of my friends. I'm afraid one day I won't be able to leave my home.

I don't know what causes this. I feel like I'm having a heart attack. My heart starts beating so fast, my whole body turns into a sweaty bundle of nerves and my legs turn to rubber. It's getting so bad I can hardly go visit my relatives, let alone sit down and have a weekend dinner with them. I find myself overly depressed most of the time and I know it's because of this. I want to do so many things, but having experienced this so many, many times . . . I just can't.

I've told myself, "you are not going to let this happen," but it always does . . . and I just don't know why. I just haven't any control over it. It can happen anywhere at any time. I feel like running away. But in many situations I can't, so I stay and make a complete fool of myself. There is no way of hiding it. If I could I would. Feeling this way is one thing, but to have people see you like this is another.

Because of this I feel nervous all the time now. I haven't had a good nights sleep in so long, no doubt because it's working on my mind. I want so much to feel normal. I know this is far from normal.

I am a very good auto mechanic. I want to work, but I can't. I don't feel like a man anymore. My wife supports the family. That's supposed to be my job. I've been to many doctors, but they don't seem to understand and keep giving me pills. The pills don't help. I'm always scared.

I've read this over and it sound so stupid and crazy. But, I'm going to send this one out because I know I need help. I hope I'm not beyond help. I'm so ashamed of it. I can't talk to anyone about it besides my wife, and she looks at me like I'm crazy. Maybe I am.

Do you think you can help me? I hope so and I hope I'll be hearing from you soon.

G. H.

Three letters out of hundreds I have received. As one who has walked the road of a male agoraphobic, my heart goes out to all of them. It is not that I feel less about the female agoraphobic. It's just that many "hot buttons" are pushed in me when I read these letters. How well I remember what it was like.

Many male agoraphobics select careers that separate them from people involvements, such as writers, artists, photographers, dog groomers, accountants and other solitary professions. They do not really know why they are more comfortable in these lonely professions. They just accept it and prefer not to be involved in the interplay of the outside world. Those that are in more active professions usually remain in secure positions, refusing promotions and travel. They are usually "loners" and do not mingle with the other employees. If they are involved in a active career when the active agoraphobia strikes, they make adjustments to try to cope, such as the drinking and pill taking described earlier.

The family unit is severely affected by the husband/father being agoraphobic. Job loss, career changes and loss of income are common. Impotency affects sexual relations. Withdrawal and depression cause much concern and confusion. The very soul of the male agoraphobic is affected by the fears and limitations.

The treatment of the male agoraphobic differs from the female because the circumstances, role in life and goals of recovery are different. Any program or therapist involved must have a total and complete understanding of agoraphobia and how it affects the male. Most case histories and media exposure emphasizes the female agoraphobic. Although the cause is the same, the male's role in life, ego, expectations, family involvements, career goals and self image differ.

All of the processes and procedures in this book can be used by either male or female agoraphobics. However, I am directing this message to the male agoraphobic:

You are a man, even though you may doubt it at times. There is within you thousands of years of manliness which will give you the courage to overcome the fears that enter your life, whether external or internal.

Do not despair or feel guilty because of your limitations. You will overcome them. You were put on this earth for a reason and purpose. You have a goal to fulfill, and you will fulfill it.

Persevere in your fight for recovery. Do not give up.

Have faith in yourself. I have walked your road and beat agoraphobia. I am not special. If I can do it, so can you.

There are people that understand and CARE. Find them and join me in the freedom that I have experienced as a recovered agoraphobic. God Bless You.

The Functional Agoraphobic

14

It is a common mistake to think of all agoraphobics as homebound. In actuality, the homebound agoraphobic is the minority. A vast majority of agoraphobics are functional to some degree, some more than others.

I like to compare agoraphobics to pregnant women. It makes no difference if you are one month pregnant or nine months pregnant. Either way, you are pregnant. The difference is in the degree of pregnancy and limitations it causes.

If you took a 12″ ruler and compare the scale to the degrees of functioning for an agoraphobic, each 1/16 of an inch would be another degree of functioning. Although all are under the large umbrella called agoraphobia, all are individuals. This also applies to their degrees of functioning.

Let us define what is meant by "functional." Webster's Dictionary defines functional as "The normal or characteristic action of anything." It goes further and says, "A special duty or performance required in the course of work or activity." The first definition, "the normal or characteristic action of anything" applies to the agoraphobic if we consider the adjustments to the fear as being "normal" and "characteristic." It is the second definition that is limiting to the agoraphobic. The words "performance required" makes the difference between the functional agoraphobic and the rest of the "normal" world.

The functional agoraphobic can do some things, and cannot do others, depending on the amount of anxiety the situation or event invokes in her. For instance, she may be able to do some minor shopping in a small stores, but cannot go to a super market. She may be able to travel two miles from her home, but cannot go three.

In venturing out into the world, many functional agoraphobics can do very well, as long as they are with their support person. They can go anywhere and do anything. The difference is the sense of security they feel. The knowledge that there is a trusted person nearby to help if they suffer the dreaded panic attack alleviates the anxiety and they feel free enough to be functional.

Many people are not aware that they are in reality, functional agoraphobics. They live their lives with constant low grade anxiety and fears. This becomes their normal attitude about life and they create a safe world around them. They very rarely go places by themselves, such as restaurants or movies. They accept the fears and anxieties as "This is the way I am." They do not seek help unless life creates circumstances which lead them to the initial panic attack. Then the build up of stifled emotions and fears releases, and they become active agoraphobics.

They cannot see that they are walking time bombs. There are thousands of undiagnosed agoraphobics in the United States. It is predictable that someday they are going to make the transference to active agoraphobia.

Those agoraphobics who are diagnosed, or who diagnosed themselves, do not necessarily become homebound. They make adjustments to the fears and anxieties and become limited in their movements. They make excuses for not doing certain things they used to do. They seek help, but usually the wrong kind. They concentrate on returning to the way they used to be, not realizing that the way they used to be led them to being agoraphobic. They enter the merry-go-round of frustrations that were described earlier in this book. In a way, they are less fortunate than the homebound agoraphobic. The homebound agoraphobic has given up for a while. The functional agoraphobic is still fighting the battle. But, they have difficulty in identifying the enemy. The enemy is themselves, not the outside world.

The frustrations of functional agoraphobics are multiplied by the knowledge that they are limited for no apparent reason, except fear. They are usually in good health and do not have a physical handicap. This causes the outside world to look upon them with confusion and misunderstanding. They can do things one day and cannot do them the next. They ask the question "Why?" They are as confused as the non-agoraphobics. The reason is that the agoraphobic is not feeling the same internally (emotionally) every day and even though the situation they were successful with may be the same, their emotional "being" was not. In other words, *it* was the same, *they* were not. This is hard to accept, until you explore the circumstances of each day. Perhaps there was an argument, or they were notified of an upcoming wedding or some other "threatening" event. This immediately starts the fear cycle and the confidence and feelings of well being they had yesterday are not present today. These internal feelings change the complexion of things and they do not function as well.

Most of the traits, personalities, fears, insecurities, inadequacies and symptoms of agoraphobia are previously discussed in this book. All or part of these can be related to by the functional agoraphobic. We have also discussed therapies and techniques for moving forward from functional to recovering agoraphobic. If there is still confusion, I suggest you re-read those chapters that apply to you and your limitations. You don't have to settle for "functional" when you can be "recovered." You will note in the progression of agoraphobia below, it is just two steps from functional to recovered.

The Progression of Agoraphobia

The latent agoraphobic—One who has the agoraphobic traits and is living a limited life or not functioning to his/her full potential. This could be one of the thousands of undiagnosed agoraphobics.

The active agoraphobic—This usually takes place after the first panic attack. The lifestyle becomes more limited because of the fear of the panic attack reoccuring.

The functional agoraphobic—One who has had the panic attack, but is fighting the fears and anxieties. Their life is limited, but they are not homebound.

The recovering agoraphobic—One who has come to grips with the agoraphobia and is developing new techniques and attitudes to deal with life. This person is taking risks.

The recovered agoraphobic—One who has finally come to the realization that agoraphobia needn't be part of his or her life. He or she has developed positive attitudes and knows he or she can handle any situation that may be encountered.

It takes proper therapy and the ability to take the necessary risks to make the transition from functional to recovering to recovered. I know I am making it sound simple. The truth is, it's not as hard as you may think. With the proper guidance, you can travel the road to recovery using longer and longer strides. It is your responsibility to find the therapy that works for you. It is available if you seek it out.

There are many roads to recovery and there is one for you. Find it and enjoy the journey.

The Homebound
Agoraphobic

15

If the media had a friend, it would be the homebound agoraphobic. They love to write about her. She is shown in illustrations and photographs as a sad looking woman, peering through her venetian blinds at the world outside. The accompanying story will tell of a person that has spent 10 (20, 30) years in her home because of this strange malady called agoraphobia.

The homebound agoraphobic has been written about to such a great extent that the public believes that all agoraphobics are homebound. Unfortunately, many professional therapists also believe this, and often, more functional agoraphobics are told, "You cannot be agoraphobic. You can leave your home."

If a person were suffering from a physical disease or handicap and remained at home, it would not be thought of as strange. Why then, if a person is suffering from a severe fear, does it seem so strange that she would remain where she feels safe? It seems to me that this would be the most "normal" thing to do.

I have worked with many homebound agoraphobics throughout the years. Many are not as unhappy with their plight as you might think. They make adjustments to their circumstances. They find ways to keep busy and many have home businesses that create income. They are wonderful homemakers and mothers, even though they cannot participate in their children's outside activities.

I am not saying that ALL homebound agoraphobics are content with their lot in life. I am saying that many have adjusted to this situation because they have given up. They have tried to venture forth with disastrous results. The fear, pain and insecurity they felt when leaving their "safe place" did not justify continuing trying.

I have illustrated this in a previous chapter, comparing the homebound agoraphobic to a person being hit with a baseball bat when she left her home. No "normal" person would subject themselves to being continually hit with a baseball bat when she left home. Why is it thought of as abnormal not to want to suffer extreme fear when leaving her "safe place?"

The lack of understanding is created by the fact that most non-agoraphobics cannot relate to fear being so strong. They have never experienced that level of fear. They have never had their bodies react in such violent ways that they felt the hand of death upon them. They have never had just a thought create physical symptoms of weakness and shuddering. They do not know the reactions that negative anticipation can create in the agoraphobic. The homebound agoraphobic is doing what is best for her at the time. She is surviving under adverse circumstances.

I am writing this, not to encourage becoming homebound, but to let the reader know that these people are not "crazy." What they are doing is "normal" for them. They are intelligent, sensitive human beings who need understanding. It is their choice to remain where they feel safe. Underlying is the same need for self preservation anyone would have by not going outside during a hurricane or tornado. If someone tried to force you out during a hurricane, they would be accused of being cruel and heartless. It is cruel and heartless to try to force a homebound agoraphobic to leave their "safe area" when they are not ready to do so.

Careful preparation must be made before the homebound agoraphobic will be ready to cross the threshold. Remember, they are facing going into the lions den. They must be prepared.

First, there must be an understanding of why they have remained homebound. They have experienced extreme fear and panic when "out in the world" and have come to believe that "something out there" is causing this. Therefore, they are remaining where they feel safe. This does not mean that they have not experienced anxiety and panic at home. They may have, but they also know that they are in a safe environment and can deal with it better. In some cases, one room of the house will be safe and another will not be. I have worked with a woman who spent 8 years in a large walk in closet. This was the only room in her house in which she felt secure and did not suffer anxiety. It is this fear of re-experiencing the dreaded panic attack that keeps this person homebound.

Secondly, do not think that all that has to be done is to reassure them that you are with them and if they hold your hand it will be all right. It's not that simple. They have to have an ironclad guarantee that they will not feel anxiety or panic when they leave their safe environment. That guarantee can only come when they develop a new mental attitude which assures them that, even if they do feel anxiety, they can handle it. This takes preparation. It takes confidence, and, above all, it takes extreme courage. The level of motivation to leave has to be very high. There has to be such a level of discontent in remaining in their safe environment, that it is worth the risk to suffer the pain they anticipate.

I counseled a woman who was homebound for 14 years. She adjusted to her situation so well, that anything she needed or wanted was just a phone call away. She did not lack for material things, but her friends and relatives have given up on her. She needed human companionship. That was the motivator I needed. She realized that she had something to offer society and her new purpose in life was to share herself and to be of service to others. It took a year, but I will never forget the joy she shared with me when she walked through the doorway that imprisoned her for all those years. She was well prepared for the event, and her eldest son was with her. He was also prepared and realized that at any time, she could panic and return to her safety. She did not do so. She went out into the sunshine. An interesting side note is that she was in her seventies at the time.

Motivation is strange. What motivates one will not motivate another. A wise therapist will spend the time necessary to know his patient and develop a high level of trust. I believe you have to be more of a friend than counselor. The innermost feelings and dreams must be known by the therapist so that the direction of motivation will be solid. I have known a home-bound agoraphobic who refused to leave a building that was on fire because of the fear of crossing her doorway. Fortunately, the fire was put out before it reached her apartment. She would rather have died than leave. Saving her life was not motivating enough. The "hot buttons" have to be found and used. This takes creativity and patience on the part of the therapist.

Thirdly, there has to be total understanding of the homebound agoraphobic's reasons for not leaving her "safe place." All of the logical explanations and reasons to leave will fall upon deaf ears. Logic has nothing to do with emotions, and the fear is emotional. Trying to convince an agoraphobic that what he or she is doing is irrational, without understanding them thoroughly, will not accomplish the goal. They KNOW they are being rational by avoiding the feared panic attack. Without understanding, you both will be frustrated and nothing will be accomplished. If they trust you enough, they will tell you the fears and fantasies that they feel they will face if they leave. Use this information wisely. It is the key to the prison.

Fourth, be aware that most homebound agoraphobics have adjusted to their environment. Any other environment will feel strange to them. They have to have assurances that what they are to face is also safe. They have to have areas of security available to them, if needed. Would you drive 3000 miles across country on a route that does not have any service stations? Of course not. It is the same with an agoraphobic, particularly one who is facing the world for the first time in years.

Fifth, do not expect the homebound agoraphobic to walk across that threshold until THEY are ready to do so, not when you expect or demand that they do so. They are taking the risk, not you. And it is a risk. To me, the homebound agoraphobic who goes to her mailbox for the first time has as much or more courage than the first man who walked on the moon.

There are many homebound agoraphobics who are experiencing a living hell. They do not get the relief from the anxiety attacks at home and suffer continuously. They will be bedbound or function at minimal levels. Their family is angry and frustrated by the dilemma. Perhaps her husband is tired of carrying the responsibilities of being both husband and homemaker. Her feelings of guilt magnify her symptoms. She is usually afraid to be left alone, and family adjustments have to be made for her. This is a much more difficult situation to deal with than the homebound agoraphobic who feels safe in her environment.

The most important factor in helping the anxious homebound agoraphobic is understanding. The more understanding she receives, the more encouraged she will be to deal with her limitations. If she were suffering from terminal cancer, she would get all of the understanding and sympathy in the world. Many sufferers of agoraphobia would gladly trade places with a cancer patient because of this attitude.

The understanding must be combined with patience. In this case, patience is not only a virtue, it is a necessity. Any movement in a positive direction, no matter how small or insignificant, must be affirmed and encouraged. Keep in mind the levels of fear she is dealing with. Any risk must be taken be her, and her alone. You can be there for support, but she is feeling the fear and must overcome it. Patience, support and understanding will encourage her to take the risks necessary to break out of her prison.

It is not unusual for the homebound agoraphobic to use alcohol to relieve her symptoms. The tendency to become an alcoholic is there. Professional guidance should be sought if this seems to be a problem. DO NOT try to take away her alcohol without this guidance. You would be pulling a life preserver away from a drowning person.

The same applies to medication. If there is an addictive problem, DO NOT try to handle it without professional guidance from one who is trained in dealing with substance abuse.

The thought processes of the homebound agoraphobic are not much different than those of any other agoraphobic. The difference is in the adjustment made in handling the fears and symptoms. You can be a prisoner in your home, or you can be a prisoner in a large geographic area. Either way, you are limited in your movements. There is more involved in the treatment of the homebound agoraphobic, but basically, the treatment is the same as any other sufferer.

Finally, be aware that becoming homebound is an adjustment to extreme fear. Those inner feelings of fear must be dealt with before the risk of leaving the safe environment is experienced.

A large percentage of the agoraphobics who have contacted the New Beginning Foundation were homebound when they started the recovery process. With understanding, caring, patience and good counseling, they are now functional members of society.

Have faith. Your time will come.

The Support Person, Family and Friends   **16**

The role of being the support person for an agoraphobic can be very frustrating, confusing and time consuming. The relationship is that of parent and child, except that the child is an adult and the parent is usually a spouse. This often leads to conflicts, since the support person is usually not prepared to relate to another adult as one who is dealing with life with childlike emotions. An appropriate phrase to describe the role of the support person in one sentence is "You're damned if you do . . . and you're damned if you don't."

My wife, Rosemary was my support person for many years while I was actively agoraphobic. I could not leave the house without her, with the exception of going to my office, which I handled by making many adjustments. All her activities were limited because of my affliction. She had to call me if she left the house while I was at work to tell me where she was going, how long she would be there, if there was an available phone number and when she would be back. She always would check in with me upon her return. This procedure would be followed even if she was going to visit a friend or going shopping for dinner. If she was going to spend some time in the yard, away from the phone, she would call me and let me know that she was at home, but unable to hear the phone if I called. She was an agoraphobic by proxy, being limited in her movements because of my condition.

After my recovery I often asked her why she did it . . . why she stayed with me during my illness. The answer was always, "Because I loved you and felt committed to you." I realize now that this was the only answer that made sense, since the role of the support person is one that could be thankless, limiting and is certainly a full time job.

Since the support person is the most important person in the agoraphobic's life, he or she has many responsibilities over and above those expected in a "normal" relationship. In the role of parent, he has to adjust to a childlike dependency in the relationship. This can cause a strain on the relationship if the support person is not aware of the reasons for the dependency and how to handle it.

The reasons for the dependency are explained in this book and should be read by the support person as well as the agoraphobic. Accepting that the agoraphobic is relating to life with childlike emotions, fears and attitudes will help the support person in adjusting to the actions of the agoraphobic and take some strain off of the relationship.

However, it is important for the agoraphobic to know that the support person will never really understand and it is unreasonable for the agoraphobic to expect him to. An analogy would be expecting a male to understand what it is like to give birth. Unless you have personally had the experience, all the words, books and lectures would be only an intellectual exercise. It is the same for the agoraphobic and the support person.

Since truly understanding the condition by the support person is an unreasonable expectation, then another direction should be considered that will help the situation. That is for the support person to *ACCEPT* that what the agoraphobic is experiencing is *REAL*. It is not a lifestyle the agoraphobic desires by choice. They want to be independent, functional human beings and not suffer the pain and agony of agoraphobia. They are not shirking their responsibilities as has been suggested in other publications. They are as frustrated, angry and confused as the support person is.

In order to be a "true" support person, there are some guidelines which I recommend be followed:

1. *ACCEPT* the actions and words of the agoraphobic without questioning. She is also confused and may not be able to explain her feelings and fears. Just *ACCEPT* that they are real. Questioning will only magnify the feelings and make matters worse.

2. Do not think that logic will overcome emotions. It is like mixing oil and water. They will never blend. By stating "There is nothing to fear." when she feels fearful, you are negating her feelings and this causes great frustration. She is thinking, "How do I get him to understand what I am going through?" All the logical words in the world will not alter the situation.

3. Remember that your role is one of "parent." If you are a critical parent, you are going to be dealing with an angry "child." Try being a nurturing parent at times when the agoraphobic is feeling the fear. Hold her as if she were a needy child and tell her that it is going to be alright. You will be amazed at how quickly the fear will dispel and the agoraphobic feels more relaxed.

4. If the agoraphobic is fearful of being left alone, make accommodations to that fear. Find a trusted person to be with the agoraphobic if you are not going to be available. Do not expect her to adjust to being left alone. The fear is too great. If accommodations are made, you can leave with a

clear conscience. If the agoraphobic were a physically ill person and bed bound, you would not leave her without a nurse. The situation is the same, She is as needy as that ill person.

5. Try to be patient. Encourage the agoraphobic to take some small risks when she is ready, but do not push her. Affirm your support, but let the choice be hers. She is the one who has to handle the fear, not you.

6. Hear what is being said and do not ask why, even if it does not make sense to you. If you are going for a ride, and she says "turn back," do it. If you go further, you will create anxiety and mistrust.

7. Do not try to force the agoraphobic to do something she is not ready for. If you do, it will surely end in failure. Be aware of the limitations and work around them. Let the agoraphobic tell you what is needed to face a risky situation and then fulfill those needs.

8. Even if you do not understand the reactions created by agoraphobia, be sympathetic. This is not to be confused with pity. By showing that you are *trying* to understand, the agoraphobic will feel more secure.

9. Affirm her successes and let her know that you are pleased and proud of her. There are no small or great successes in the eyes of the agoraphobic. Any positive accomplishment should be affirmed.

10. Do not chide her for any failures. Tell them that next time it will be better and you are proud that she tried.

11. Be aware of the agoraphobic's "comfort level." If you sense she is uncomfortable when you are out, suggest leaving. Then, let her make the choice. In many cases she will stay and be more comfortable, knowing you are aware of her feelings.

12. Avoid accusations. The agoraphobic feels very insecure as it is, and by accusing her of anything, the insecurity is magnified.

13. Do not ignore her. Let her share her feelings with you. In many cases she does not have anyone else to listen to her. Be considerate of her need to talk.

14. Even though the agoraphobic is limited, do not leave her out of family plans. She has to feel included and needed. Let the decision of whether or not to participate be hers.

All of the above can be a strain on the support person. It can be handled with love and consideration or with anger and resentment. I know it is not easy. However, there is a payoff. The agoraphobic will be easier to live with, be happier and more secure and will develop the confidence and trust needed to attempt recovery.

There is an erroneous belief that by accommodating the limitations of agoraphobia, you are prolonging the problem. This is not true. You would not expect a "child" to face the world without being prepared to do so. They have to develop confidence and know that they are supported. It is the same with the agoraphobic. Before they can "grow" out of agoraphobia, they must be ready to do so. The dependency can only change when they feel independent, and this can only happen when they feel secure.

The entire family is affected by the agoraphobic member and accommodations and concessions must be made. There is no question that there is a strain on the family unit. It is interesting that children are more accepting of the limitations of agoraphobia than adults. This is probably due to the fact that as children, their emotional makeup is similar to that of the agoraphobic and they can relate easier to the feelings. However, they are aware that mommy or daddy is different than other parents and may not be able to participate in the things other parents do. I feel it is a mistake not to tell the children that mommy or daddy has a problem. It is worse for the child to be confused by not knowing that a problem exists and that there are reasons for the parent to be "different."

Friends can act as support people as well as spouses and family. The same rules apply and if they are to be support persons, they should become as familiar with the problem as those directly involved with it. Reading this book can be of great help in this direction.

A Special Note to the Agoraphobic

Please be aware that your support person has needs and feelings also. They are confused and frustrated by your condition. You have to be supportive of them as well as they being supportive of you. It is only right that you try to understand their position and realize that it is not easy for them. Remember the golden rule, "Do unto others as you would have them do unto you." Listen to their side of the story as you would like them to listen to yours. Try to make adjustments in your lifestyle so that they can have some time for themselves. Be the best wife, husband, mother, father, friend you can be. The more mutual understanding and acceptance you have for each other, the easier it is going to be for all.

A Special Note to the Support People, Family and Friends

The agoraphobic in your life needs your acceptance and support. Think of him or her as an emotionally fearful, insecure child when in need of you and act accordingly. He or she has no one else to turn to when reacting to the emotional fears, insecurities and frustrations. Even though it may not be easy, have compassion for his or her circumstances and do your best to be there for support.

It is not a hopeless situation. With the proper help, he or she will get well again and your relationship will be even stronger. Your love and concern is the best medicine that can be received.

You also will feel frustration and confusion. Do not give in to these feelings. Your strength is needed. Share it with your agoraphobic.

ACCEPT that the feelings and fears are real to the agoraphobic. They are not trying to get attention or avoid responsibility.

Above all, do not give up. When it is all over and the agoraphobic is recovered, he or she will be the best spouse, parent or friend you will ever have.

Drugs, Alcohol and Nutrition

17

While I was actively agoraphobic, I was used as a guinea pig by a psychiatrist I was seeing. Every time a detail man from a drug company presented a new barbituate, sedative or tranquilizer to him, I was the one he would use to test the drug. I suppose the reasons were I was the only agoraphobic he was treating and I would take anything to relieve the anxiety. If he told me to put cow dung in my left ear and hop on my right foot, and that would relieve the anxiety and fear I was feeling. . . . I would have been stuffing and hopping without hesitation.

The 1950's, a new miracle drug . . . the tranquilizer . . . was introduced. It was to be the answer to all our problems. The miracle drug was called Miltown. It was yesterday's Valium and Xanax. The medical community hailed it as the best thing since pop-up tissues. Miltown was supposed to be my salvation.

I must admit it did have a marked effect on me. It was so effective that I became a walking vegetable. It is true, the feelings of anxiety decreased, but so did all other feelings. I remember being in the waiting room when my daughter was born. I had been taking Miltowns like they were Lifesavers. I didn't know where I was or why. My father-in-law and mother-in-law were with me at the time. After the doctor called down from the delivery room to inform me that I was a proud father of a daughter, I returned to my seat, but didn't even have the ability to absorb the news, and so, neglected to tell my in-laws that my wife had given birth. After a while my father-in-law asked who called. It was then that I informed them they were grandparents.

I also found that alcohol would make me feel less anxious, so I had a few drinks at night after work. As added security, I kept a flask in my car, just in case I needed it while I was away from home.

Unfortunately, as drugged as I was, the fear and depression still seeped through. I felt that if one Miltown was good, then two or three would be even better. I was convinced that medication was the answer. After all, they were prescribed by my doctor and he assured me these "magic" pills would take care of the problem.

For many years I dutifully swallowed the new drugs as they were introduced on the market, hoping that each new pill would make me "normal" again. Of course, they did not do what I wanted them to . . . but . . . many did make me feel less anxious. I despaired that this was going to be my life, taking pills and living in a daze.

In retrospect, I do not blame my doctor or myself for creating a dependence upon drugs. There weren't any other answers available except psychiatric counseling and that did not relieve the fears and anxiety. Medication was the only other way to approach the condition.

Thirty years later it seems that the only progress that has been made for agoraphobics is in the availability of new drugs. The lack of research into the condition and it's proper treatment has left the agoraphobic with the same choices I had so long ago. In my opinion, the medical, psychiatric and psychological communities have neglected their responsibility to the public by not accepting the seriousness of the problem and being more aware that there are millions who are suffering and needy of proper help.

There are many agoraphobics who are fearful of taking drugs. It is a fear of addiction, of altering the mind, loss of control and unknown side effects which hampers drug therapies for these people. If three 5 mg. Valium's are prescribed to be taken each day, many agoraphobics will take only ½ of one pill, and then only when they are desperate. However, on the other side of the coin, many are like I was believing that if some is good, more is better.

Please understand, I am not in any way anti-medication. I do not feel that medication alone is the answer, but should be used as an adjunct while seeking the answer. A good drug therapy program, well monitored, combined with a good counseling program, such as we offer at the New Beginning Foundation, can be very effective.

When a chemical is introduced into the body, the individual response may differ from person to person. The effects of the medication may vary and your doctor may have to experiment to find the drug which will work best for you. It is important that you keep the doctor informed of your reactions and any relief you may get from your medication.

Medication should be used as part of your therapy, not as the total solution. Relieving the anxiety does not remove the fear, and, it is the fear that keeps you limited. Drugs may allow you to be more functional and that can give you the opportunity to seek other help to deal with the causes of agoraphobia and work towards your recovery.

The following information is taken from the Physicians Desk Reference, a publication that is available at any library. It lists all available drugs and their side effects. It might be a handy reference guide to have at home, or you could call the library for specific drug information. I will list some of the more commonly prescribed drugs that are used for the treatment of anxiety and the other symptoms of agoraphobia, and their side effects. This is being done for your information only.

Special Note

If you are highly suggestible or susceptible, I do not advise that you read the side effects listed below. They may make you extra wary when taking any medication. All drug use prescription or non-prescription, should be discussed with your physician or therapist, including side effects and benefits.

ADAPIN—SEE SINEQUAN

ALPRAZOLAM—SEE XANAX

ATARAX—This drug is a sedative. It is also used for the relief of itching caused by allergies.
Side effects are: drowsiness, dry mouth, chest tightness, convulsions, breathing difficulties, sore throat, tremors.
It is not to be used in conjunction with other depressants or alcohol.

ATIVAN—This drug is a sedative and hypnotic. It is commonly used for the relief of tension, anxiety, insomnia, agitation and irritability.
Side effects are: Headache, nausea, unsteadiness, blurred vision, change in appetite, diarrhea, depression, constipation, dry mouth, dizziness, increased salivation, drowsiness, rash, weakness, slurred speech, sore throat, decreased hearing, difficult breathing, disorientation, fever, hallucinations, eye function disturbance, menstrual irregularities, palpitations, jaundice.
It is not to be used if you are taking other medications with sedative properties nor with alcohol. It also interacts with other types of drugs. Your doctor should be made aware of all drugs being taken with Ativan.

BARBPIL—SEE PHENOBARBITAL

BARBITA—SEE PHENOBARBITAL

BARMATE—SEE MEPROBAMATE

BUTABARBITAL—SEE BUTISOL SODIUM

BUTATRAN—SEE BUTISOL SODIUM

BUTAZEM—SEE BUTISOL SODIUM

BUTISOL SODIUM—This drug is a sedative and hypnotic drug and is used for anxiety, tension and insomnia.
Side effects are: Sore throat, rash, excitement, depression, clumsiness, chest tightness, confusion, difficult breathing, jaundice, slurred speech, vomiting, nausea, headache, drowsiness, diarrhea, constipation, dizziness, hangover, joint pain, stomach upset.

It should not be used for those with an overactive adrenal gland or by those that have a sensitivity to aspirin. It interacts with alcohol and other drugs. Your doctor should be made aware of all drugs being taken with Butisol Sodium.

CENTRAX—This is a sedative and hypnotic drug and is used for the treatment of anxiety.

Side effects are: Confusion, depression, dizziness, dry mouth, fatigue, heartburn, nausea, sweating, vomiting, rash, loss of appetite, headache, excess saliva, drowsiness, diarrhea, constipation, blurred vision, difficult urination, excitement, hallucinations, low blood pressure, rapid heart rate, sore throat, tremors, uncoordinated movements, stimulation, slurred speech, menstrual irregularities, jaundice, fever, double vision, difficult breathing.

Do not take this drug with alcohol, central nervous system drugs or oral anti-coagulants. This drug is very habit forming.

COPROBATE—SEE MEPROBAMATE

DALMANE—This is a hypnotic drug and is generally used for insomnia.

Side effects are: Bitter taste in mouth, constipation, depression, diarrhea, dizziness, drowsiness, dry mouth, fatigue, flushing, headache, heartburn, loss of appetite, nausea, nervousness, rash, sweating, vomiting, blurred vision, chest pain, depression, difficult urination, double vision, fainting, falling, jaundice, joint pain, low blood pressure, mouth sores, nightmares, palpitations, shortness of breath, slurred speech, sore throat, stimulation, uncoordinated moves.

You are not to take this drug is you have impaired liver or kidney function, lung disease or myasthenia gravis. Do not take with alcohol, central nervous system drugs or oral anti-coagulants.

EDEBAMATE—SEE MEPROBAMATE

ELAVIL—This drug is an anti-depressant and is used for the relief of depression.

Side effects are: Agitation, black tongue, blurred vision, confusion, constipation, cramps, diarrhea, dizziness, drowsiness, dry mouth, fatigue, headache, heartburn, sensitivity to light, insomnia, loss of appetite, nausea, peculiar tastes, rash, restlessness, sweating, vomiting, weakness, bleeding, convulsions, difficult urination, enlarged or painful breasts, fainting, fever, fluid retention, hair loss, hallucinations, heart attack, high or low blood pressure, imbalance, impotence, jaundice, mood changes, mouth sores, nervousness, nightmares, numbness in fingers or toes, palpitations, psychosis, ringing in ears, sleep disorders, sore throat, stroke, tremors, uncoordinated movements, weight loss or gain.

Do not take this drug if you have glaucoma, heart disease, high blood pressure, enlarged prostate, epilepsy, urine retention, liver disease, hyperthyroidism, or if you are undergoing electroshock therapy or surgery. It interacts with many drugs, including oral anti-coagulants and oral contraceptives. It should not be taken if you are taking any over-the-counter drugs for cough, cold or sinus problems. It can also cause sudden mood swings or green colored urine. It should not be taken with alcohol.

EQUANIL—SEE MEPROBAMATE

ETRAFON—SEE TRIAVIL

EVENOL—SEE MEPROBAMATE

HENOTAL—SEE PHENOBARBITAL

IMIPRAMINE—SEE TOFRANIL

INFADORM—SEE PHENOBARBITAL

LIBRIUM—This is a sedative and hypnotic drugs used for the relief of anxiety, nervousness, tension, muscle spasms, withdrawal symptoms of alcohol addiction.

Side effects are: Blood disorders, blurred vision, decrease or increase of sex drive, difficult breathing, difficult urination, double vision, excitation, fever, hallucinations, jaundice, low blood pressure, slow heart rate, slurred speech, sore throat, stimulation, tremors, confusion, constipation, depression, dizziness, drooling, drowsiness, dry mouth, fainting, fatigue, fluid retention, headache, heartburn, insomnia, loss of appetite, menstrual irregularities, nausea, rash, sweating.

This drug should not be used by people who have liver problems, kidney disease, glaucoma, or are depressed, It should not be used with other nervous system drugs or alcohol. Blood count and liver function tests should be taken regularly when using this drug.

LIMBITROL—This is an anti-depressant used for the treatment of depression and anxiety.

Side effects are: Agitation, black tongue, bloating, blurred vision, confusion, constipation, cramps, diarrhea, dizziness, drowsiness, dry mouth, fatigue, headache, heartburn, increased sensitivity to light, insomnia, loss of appetite, nasal congestion, nausea, numbness in fingers or toes, peculiar tastes, rash, restlessness, stomach upset, sweating, vomiting, weakness, bleeding, convulsions, difficult urination, enlarged or painful breasts, fainting, fever, fluid retention, hair loss, hallucinations, heart attack, high or low blood pressure, imbalance, impotence, jaundice, menstrual irregularities, mood changes, mouth sores, nervousness, nightmares, palpitations, psychosis, ringing in ears, sleep disorders, sore throat, stroke, tremors, uncoordinated movements, weight loss or gain.

This drug should not be taken by those people who are using monoamine oxidase inhibitors, have glaucoma, lung disease, high blood pressure, myasthenia gravis, enlarged prostate, intestinal blockage, heart disease, epilepsy, thyroid disease, liver or kidney disease, urinary retention. It should not be taken with alcohol or other sedative drugs or while taking drugs for cough, cold or sinus problems. It may change blood sugar levels.

LUMINAL OVOIDS—SEE PHENOBARBITAL

MEPRIAM—SEE MEPROBAMATE

MEPROBAMATE—This is a sedative or hypnotic drug which is used for anxiety and insomnia.

Side effects are: Asthma, bruising, clumsiness, convulsions, difficult breathing, euphoria, fainting, fever, fluid retention, kidney damage, low blood pressure, nightmares, numbness or tingling, palpitations, slurred speech, sore throat, stimulation, blurred vision, diarrhea, dizziness, dry mouth, headache, nausea, rash, vomiting and weakness.

This drug should not be used by people with epilepsy or kidney disease or with alcohol or other sedative drugs.

MILTOWN—SEE MEPROBAMATE

NARDIL—This is a monamine oxidase (MAO) inhibitor. It is used in the treatment of depression.

Side effects are: Fainting, severe headache, dizziness, hallucinations, insomnia, nightmares, rash, dry mouth, diarrhea, constipation, nausea, vomiting, rapid or pounding heartbeat, chest pain, stiff neck, difficult urination, fatigue, weakness.

Do not take this drug with non-prescription diet pills, nose drops, medicine for asthma, cough, cold or allergy, or medicine containing caffeine or alcohol. Should not be taken with foods containing tyramine. This drug should be carefully monitored by your physician.

NEURAMATE—SEE MEPROBAMATE

PHENOBARBITAL—This is a sedative and hypnotic drug used to control convulsions, anxiety or tension and sleep disorders.

Side effects are: Allergic reactions, breathing difficulty, bruising, chest tightness, confusion, excitation, loss of coordination, low blood pressure, slow heart rate, slurred speech, diarrhea, dizziness, drowsiness, headache, muscle pain, nausea, stomach upset and vomiting.

Do not take if you have a liver disease or lung disease. It should not be taken with alcohol, other depressants, oral contraceptives and other drugs. Your doctor should be made aware of all medications you are taking, whether prescription or not.

PHENOSQUAR—SEE PHENOBARBITAL

PROTRAN—SEE MEPROBAMATE

SARISOL—SEE BUTISOL SODIUM

SECONAL—SEE BUTISOL SODIUM

SEDADROPS—SEE PHENOBARBITAL

SERAX—This is a sedative and hypnotic drug used for the relief of anxiety, nervousness, tension, muscle spasms, and withdrawal from alcohol addiction.

Side effects are: Blurred vision, decreased or increased sexual drive, difficult breathing, euphoria, excitement, fainting, fever, fluid retention, hallucinations, jaundice, menstrual irregularities, palpitations, slurred speech, sore throat, tremors, uncoordinated movements, confusion, constipation, depression, diarrhea, dizziness, drooling, drowsiness, dry mouth, fatigue, headache, heartburn, nausea, rash and sweating.

This drug should not be used by people with lung disease, epilepsy, porphyria, kidney disease, myasthenia gravis, or people with blood pressure or heart problems. Do not take with alcohol or other sedatives.

SINEQUAN—This is an anti-depressant used for depression and anxiety.

Side effects are: Bleeding, chills, convulsions, difficult urination, enlarged or painful breasts, fainting, fever, fluid retention, hair loss, hallucinations, heart attack, high or low blood pressure, imbalance, impotence, jaundice, mood changes, mouth sores, nervousness, nightmares, numbness in fingers or toes, palpitations, psychosis, ringing in the ears, severe mental disorders, sore throat, stroke, testicular swelling, tremors, uncoordinated movements, weight loss or gain, agitation, anxiety, black tongue, blurred vision, change in urine color, confusion, constipation, cramps, diarrhea, dizziness, drowsiness, dry mouth, fatigue, headache, heartburn, sensitivity to light, insomnia, loss of appetite, nausea, peculiar tastes, rash, restlessness, stomach upset, sweating, vomiting and weakness.

Do not take this drug if you have glaucoma, high blood pressure, liver or kidney disease, epilepsy, thyroid disease, peptic ulcer, enlarged prostate or intestinal blockage. It interacts with alcohol and other sedatives and drugs. Inform your physician if you have any unusual symptoms.

SK-PHENOBARBITAL—SEE PHENOBARBITAL

SODUBEN—SEE BUTISOL SODIUM

SOLFOTON—SEE PHENOBARBITAL

THORAZINE—This drug is used for the management of certain psychotic disorders, treatment of intracable hiccups, nausea and vomiting.

Side effects are: Blood disorders, breast enlargement, bruising, convulsions, darkened skin, difficulty in swallowing or breathing, fever, heart attack, impotence, involuntary movements of the face, mouth, jaw and tongue, jaundice, low or high blood sugar, palpitations, psychosis, sleep disorders, sore throat, uncoordinated movements, visual disturbances, constipation, decreased sweating, diarrhea, discoloration of the urine, dizziness, drooling, drowsiness, dry mouth, fainting, fatigue, jitteriness, low blood pressure, menstrual irregularities, nasal congestion, rash, restlessness, sun sensitivity, tremors, vomiting, weight gain.

This drug should not be used to persons allergic to phenotiazine, with heart, liver or lung disease, glaucoma, diabetes, epilepsy, brain disease, glaucoma, Parkinsons disease, breast cancer, enlarged prostate, or blockage of the urinary or digestive tracts.

Certain foods and other drugs should not be used when taking this drug. Consult with your physician.

TOFRANIL—This drug is an anti-depressant. It is also used to control bed wetting.

Side effects are: Bleeding, convulsions, difficult urination, enlarged or painful breasts, fainting, fever, fluid retention, hair loss, hallucinations, heart attack, high or low blood pressure, imbalance, impotence, jaundice, mood changes, mouth sores, nervousness, psychosis, nightmares, numbness in fingers or toes, palpitations, ringing in the ears, sleep disorders, sore throat, stroke, testicular swelling, tremors, uncoordinated movements, weight loss or gain, agitation, anxiety, black tongue, blurred vision, confusion, constipation, cramps, diarrhea, dizziness, drowsiness, dry mouth, fatigue, flushing, headache, heartburn, increased sensitivity to light, insomnia, loss of appetite, nausea, peculiar tastes, rash, restlessness, stomach upset, sweating, urine color change, vomiting, weakness.

This drug interacts with many other drugs and should be taken only upon investigation of your drug use by your physician. It should not be taken by people who have glaucoma, high blood pressure, enlarged prostate, porphyria, intestinal blockage, heart disease, epilepsy, thyroid disease, liver or kidney disease or people who receive electroshock therapy. It will also interact with alcohol, oral contraceptives and anti-coagulants.

TRANMEP—SEE MEPROBAMATE

TRIAVIL—This is an anti-depressant drug and is used for the relief of anxiety and depression.

Side effects are: Aching or numbness in arms or legs, convulsions, difficult urination, enlarged painful breasts, eye pain, fainting, fluid retention, hair loss, heart attack, high or low blood pressure, high or low blood sugar, imbalance, impotence, insomnia, involuntary movements of the face, mouth, jaw or tongue, jaundice, mouth sores, muscle stiffness, nervousness, nightmares, palpitations, ringing in the ears, sore throat, stroke, swelling of the testicles, tremors, weight loss or gain, anxiety, black tongue, blurred vision, change in urine color, confusion, constipation, decreased sweating, diarrhea, dizziness, drooling, drowsiness, dry mouth, excitement, fatigue, headache, menstrual irregularities, nasal congestion, nausea, peculiar taste in mouth, rash, restlessness, skin darkening, sun sensitivity, vomiting, weakness.

140

This drug should be used with caution by persons having thyroid disease, glaucoma, impaired liver function, heart disease, epilepsy, difficult urination, intestinal blockage, high or low blood pressure, diabetes, brain disease, Parkinsons disease, peptic ulcer, enlarged prostate, breast cancer, asthma or other respiratory disorders. This drug can affect the elevation or lowering of blood sugar. Do not take this drug with alcohol or other drugs without consulting your doctor.

TRANXENE—This is a sedative and hypnotic drug used for the relief of anxiety, nervousness, tension and withdrawal from alcohol addiction.

Side effects are: Blurred vision, depression, difficult breathing, difficult swallowing, difficult urination, double vision, fever, hallucinations, jaundice, low blood pressure, menstrual irregularities, palpitations, slow heart beat, slurred speech, sore throat, stimulation, tremors, confusion, constipation, diarrhea, dizziness, drooling, drowsiness, dry mouth, fatigue, headache, heartburn, insomnia, irritability, loss of appetite, nausea, nervousness, rash, sweating, vomiting.

This drug is not recommended for people who are severely depressed, have severe mental illness, glaucoma, liver or kidney disease, epilepsy, porphyria or myasthenia gravis. Do not use with alcohol or other sedatives. Blood counts and liver functions should be taken frequently.

VALIUM—This drug is a sedative and hypnotic and is used for the relief of anxiety, nervousness, tension, muscle spasms, and withdrawal from alcohol addiction. It is one of the most widely used drugs.

Side effects are: Blurred vision, difficult breathing, difficult urination, double vision, excitement, fever, hallucinations, jaundice, low blood pressure, menstrual irregularities, palpitations, slurred speech, sore throat, stimulation, tremors, uncoordinated movements, confusion, constipation, depression, diarrhea, dizziness, drowsiness, dry mouth, excess saliva, fatigue, headache, heartburn, loss of appetite, nausea, rash, sweating, vomiting.

This drug should not be taken by people who have severe mental illness, epilepsy, respiratory problems, myasthenia gravis, porphyria, impaired kidney or liver functions, or a history of drug abuse. It should be avoided by pregnant women and the elderly. It should not be taken with alcohol or other depressants.

XANAX—This drug is a tranquilizer and is still experimental. It is used widely in the treatment of agoraphobia.

Side effects are still not known in their entirety. Those that are known are: drowsiness, headaches, light headedness, weakness, palpitations, diarrhea, nausea, constipation, nasal congestion, dry mouth, blurred vision, confusion, insomnia, clumsiness, hallucinations, depression, irritability.

This drug should not be taken by people allergic to benzodiazepine, if you have myasthenia gravis or glaucoma. It should not be taken if you are an active or recovering alcoholic. More information may be available after publication of this book. Check with your physician.

Illegal drugs, such as cocaine, marijuana, heroin and LSD should not be used by agoraphobics under any circumstances. Besides being highly addictive, the mind altering side effects can cause panic attacks.

Amphetamines and other stimulants most commonly used in diet pills should also be avoided. They can cause hyperactivity which can lead to anxiety.

ALCOHOL

Over the years, I have counseled many agoraphobics who were also alcoholic. I found there was a definite correlation between alcoholism and agoraphobia. Many of the personality traits of the alcoholic are similar to those of the agoraphobic.

For instance, many alcoholics were brought up by parents who were alcoholic. They developed the same insecurities, fears and feelings of inadequacy in their children that the parents of agoraphobics did.

As adults, these people felt isolated and are uneasy with other people, especially authority figures. To protect themselves, they become "people-pleasers." Personal criticism is very threatening to them. Because of their insecurities, they become victims of life. They have an over-developed sense of responsibility and become concerned about others rather than themselves. They have strong guilt feelings about themselves. They have compulsive personalities, over-reacting to situations and events in a negative way. They feel very inadequate and compensate by over-doing, such as becoming workaholics. They are perfectionists. They have a fear of abandonment. They only allow themselves to show emotions and feelings when under the influence of alcohol.

As you can see there are many similarities. In a family of three children brought up by the same parents, one may become agoraphobic, one alcoholic and one severely neurotic. Why one makes one adjustment and not the other is unknown.

Alcohol has been used for centuries as a depressant. It can also be a pain killer and I am sure you remember the hero taking a slug of whiskey before the bullet was removed from his shoulder. It has also become socially acceptable to take a drink when under pressure. It is not uncommon for the harried executive to have a three martini lunch. No one even comments. After all, he has great responsibilities. He only does it to relieve the pressure.

The problem is that it works. It will reduce the stress and anxiety temporarily. The key word is "temporarily." When the effect wears off, the person is left to face the realities of his life and may feel worse because of the drinking.

It also has an accumulative effect. More and more alcohol is needed to reach the same state of euphoria. There is also a dependency factor that can be developed in a short time.

The agoraphobic is desirous of relief from his symptoms and a few drinks may do it. But there is a price to pay. Not only do you have the after effects of heavy drinking, you are also very open to anxiety and panic attacks. This may encourage you to start drinking again to prevent the attacks. Soon you are in a cycle of anxiety to drinking to after effects to more drinking to more after effects, etc.

You can also become an alcoholic. The physical and psychological dependency becomes an addiction. The body needs the alcohol and the euphoric stages you want to reach demand more and more alcoholic input. It is easier to become addicted to alcohol than to drugs. Alcohol is easier to secure. You do not have to go a doctor. It is readily available at your corner store.

I am not against agoraphobics having a drink occasionally if they need it to face a threatening situation or event. I do not feel there is any difference between that and taking a pill. The effect can be the same. As with drugs, it is the over-use that creates the problems. However, you must be cautious and aware that you have a dependant personality. The key word is "moderation."

Nutrition

Because of their sensitivity to physical reactions, agoraphobics need to be more aware of proper diets than non-agoraphobics.

Much has been much written about diet and emotional responses. Many articles have promised relief from stress and anxiety advocating or avoiding certain foods and taking certain vitamins. In my personal opinion, diet does have an affect on the feelings of anxiety, but again, is not the total answer in the control or treatment of anxiety. Some vitamins are known to help relieve anxiety, since deficiencies of these vitamins have been proven to cause certain physical symptoms such as fatigue and weariness. These reactions can cause the agoraphobic to feel anxious because they may create shakey or unreal feelings which may begin the fear cycle.

B vitamin deficiency can cause fatigue, tension or depression. It is also directly involved with our energy and nervous functions. It is a water soluable vitamin and excesses are removed through the urine. It has to be replenished. A good B complex with a high grade of all the B vitamins should be part of every agoraphobic's regimen for recovery. Brewer's yeast, dessicated liver and wheat germ are excellent natural sources of B vitamins.

Coffee, tobacco and liquor can cause a deficiency of thiamine in our bodies. This deficiency can cause emotional instability, irritability, depression. a feeling of doom, fatigue, insomnia, headaches indigestion and diarrhea. White rice, white flour, sugar, chocolate and soft drinks containing caffeine can also cause a thiamine deficiency. Natural food sources of thiamine are wheat bread, beef, potatoes, polished rice, skim milk, fruit, vegetables and Brewer's yeast.

Riboflavin deficiency can cause trembling, dizziness, insomnia and mental sluggishness. The best natural sources of riboflavin are milk, liver, meat and Brewer's yeast.

Niacin deficiency can cause fearful apprehension, gloomy feelings and depression. You must be careful when using niacin supplements since it releases histamine into your system which causes the dilation of blood vessels. Niacin is found in foods high in protein.

Be aware of the signals your body sends you. If you experience an uncomfortable reaction from certain foods, avoid them. If coffee, tobacco or alcohol cause you to be shakey and irritable, eliminate them. Any physical reaction that causes the familiar feelings of anxiety can start the cycle to panic. Let your common sense be your guide. The answer to your recovery is not in your diet alone, but we must use every tool available.

A well monitored drug program, proper therapy, avoidance of those substances than can bring on the feelings of anxiety, a "common sense" diet and your desire to recover will help you overcome this condition we call agoraphobia.

The Meaning
of Recovery

18

Achieving "recovery" seems impossible or unattainable to many agoraphobics. After undergoing years of therapies which have not been successful . . . years of ups and downs (mostly downs) . . . years of non-understanding and misunderstanding of their problem . . . years of trying to overcome agoraphobia . . . it is understandable why they believe they will ever be "normal" again.

Nothing can be further from the truth. I want to assure you that recovery is not only achievable and attainable . . . it is probable if certain criteria are met. Like most things in the agoraphobic's life, recovery has become a complex topic, when in reality it is, and should be, very non-complex.

I have asked hundreds of agoraphobics to define what recovery means to them. Many have answered, "To be the way I was before I became agoraphobic." Or they say, "To not ever feel anxious and afraid again." Still others have said, "To be able to do what I want to do." As you can see, recovery is a very individual thing, each agoraphobic defining what they would like to do and how they would like to feel. The "fantasy" of recovery to the suffering agoraphobic could be a motivator or a reason to remain agoraphobic, depending on how recovery is viewed.

An agoraphobic who is severely limited, fearful and lacks self confidence, can view recovery as desirable, but very threatening. While these feelings are part of your emotional psyche, it can be frightening to imagine being able to drive the car alone, going to stores and malls alone, even being alone. The thought is, "If I recover, I will be expected to do those things . . . and I cannot conceive myself doing them. It is too frightening." What this person is doing is going from point "A" (limited agoraphobic) to point "Z" (recovered agoraphobic) in their mind, without ever experiencing the steps that have to be taken to complete the trip. They do not realize that with every step comes growth and confidence that they can handle the next portion of the trip.

The road to recovery is divided into various phases. When you start the trip, whether you are functional or homebound, you are limited, emotionally and physically. To start the trip takes great courage. There are many unknowns to be faced. Like all trips, it starts with the first step. This is going to be a "baby step," not a long stride. It is not wise to approach this trip with a "sink or swim" attitude. The goal of the first phase of the journey should be to become more functional.

To become more functional, certain techniques and attitudes must be developed. You must have proper motivation. You have to really desire to be more functional and be willing to take some small risks. Sometimes this is frightening, particularly if you have tried before and have not been successful. Develop the attitude that "This time it's going to be different. This time I am going to make it."

Techniques to control the anxiety so that you know it will never lead to panic should be learned and practiced before you start walking down the road. These techniques have been described in this book as programmed relaxation techniques which will relax you upon command. In addition, proper use of prescribed medications, and, some type of support system is desirable.

Realize that this phase of the journey to recovery is critical, since it is the foundation for the rest to follow and the foundation must be strong. Really feel and believe that if the panic attack happens, it can be diminished or controlled.

This calls for the first risk. In order to really know that you can control the anxiety, you must experience an anxious situation even though the first reaction is to avoid situations or events that might create anxiety. The time will come when life will create challenges for you. It may be a short trip, or a family gathering, or some other threatening event. This is when you must call upon your inner courage and take the first step. DO NOT try to create the first challenge by yourself. Chances are you will bite off more than you can chew. Properly prepare for the life experience, and, when it comes, GO FOR IT!

Remember, it starts with "baby steps." If you have a "safe area," the goal is to expand the area. If you feel fear and anxiety, the goal is to control those feelings to a level of comfort. That means you may go one block from your house, if leaving home is your limitation. Everything in life is relative. For someone who could not cross the threshold, one block, comfortably, is a great accomplishment. A more functional agoraphobic might be able to go to small neighborhood stores comfortably. Walking into a larger store, staying in the front for a minute, and then leaving is an accomplishment. More importantly, IT IS A START . . . and you cannot go anywhere or do anything until you start.

During this first phase of recovery, your mental attitude should be one of acceptance. That means that you realize you are handicapped by the feelings and symptoms, and will have to deal with them. Denying that you are emotionally limited can place you in situations or challenges that can cause unnecessary stress.

The Attitude of Recovery

On the road to recovery, there is no passing or failing. You will find that you are more successful if you develop an attitude of "practicing" rather than "must do." Practice means just that. Passing or failing does not apply when you practice.

This means it's OK if you accomplish your goal, and conversely, it is OK if you do not accomplish the goal. You are just practicing. You do not pass or fail. This can be a hard concept for an agoraphobic to accept.

Being perfectionists, passing is the only acceptable grade. Anything less is failure. Forget that old attitude. It only creates the negative anticipation and the accompanying anxiety which makes every challenge a major one.

Realize you have options open to you . . . that if you do not accomplish the goal the world will not end . . . you can face the challenge with less fear.

Let us create a scenario to illustrate this vital point:

Mary is an active, limited, fearful agoraphobic. She has been in counseling and feels ready to start her journey on the road to recovery. Her therapist tells her that tomorrow they are going to visit a shopping mall. This has been one of Mary's prime fears. As soon as she is told of the upcoming event, she begins to experience the fearful anxiety. That night is a living hell for her. She builds the anxiety and the fantasy of what will happen when (and if) she goes to the mall. The next morning she is a wreck, physically and emotionally. However, she knows she has to face this challenge, and, if she does not do it successfully, her therapist will be disappointed in her. Her mind focuses on two things, passing or failing. The more anxious she becomes, the more she is convincing herself that she will fail.

Her attitude of passing or failing is her downfall. She does not realize that she has options.

One option is not to go if she does not feel ready for the challenge. She may need more counseling and therapy. Only the agoraphobic knows when he or she is ready. With the proper guidance and support, she will build the confidence necessary to take the risk.

Another option is to approach the challenge as a "practicing" experience. If she goes, that's fine. If she doesn't go, that's fine too. She must realize that she has the choice. Given the choice, the levels of anticipatory anxiety will diminish.

If she does go, she must realize that she can enter the mall or not enter it. That is also her choice.

If she enters the mall, she must realize that she can stay or leave. This is also a choice.

If she leaves, she must pat herself on the back for entering and not consider this event as a failure. It was a step in the right direction and will be easier next time.

If she stays, she is to do so only as long as she is comfortable. If the anxiety level increases, she is to leave, to practice again at another time.

This is "practicing" a situation or event. Passing or failing is not part of the experience.

Confidence breeds more confidence. As your level of confidence grows, so do your self esteem and sense of worth. You have come to realize that you can accomplish more than you thought you could. This moves you to the next phase on the road to recovery . . . becoming a functional agoraphobic.

Functional agoraphobics can do more things comfortably. Their safe place has expanded and they feel a little more secure in taking risks. Many feel that when they become more functional, they are recovered. They are not, as we will learn.

Another phase of recovery is ongoing, throughout the process of recovery. That phase is called "recovering." You must go through "recovering" before you can reach "recovery."

An analogy might be in having a broken leg. When the leg breaks, you become limited (actively agoraphobic). A cast is put on the leg, and with the aid of crutches or a wheelchair, you start some movement (functional agoraphobic). The leg must take its time and heal (recovering agoraphobic). When the cast is taken off, you must start walking again with caution (ongoing recovering agoraphobic). Finally, the leg is totally healed and you are "normal" again (recovered agoraphobic).

During the recovering process, more and more challenges will enter your life. Sometimes you may feel the old fears and anxieties. However, if you have prepared yourself properly, you will overcome them with an attitude of "I can handle whatever life throws my way." This takes ongoing therapeutic support and counseling. If you are doing it on your own, it takes self affirmation.

The "recovering" phase of recovery has no time limit. You cannot force recovery, it has to happen in it's own time. Do not be discouraged by the obstacles on the road to recovery. Learning to deal with these obstacles (negativity) will teach you how to live your life as a happier, more functional person.

And so, we have gone from active to functional to recovering agoraphobic. Now we must face the ultimate . . . RECOVERY.

An important question you should ask yourself during this journey is "What are my payoffs in remaining agoraphobic?" There are payoffs, you know. These are also called "secondary gains." There is a certain security in being agoraphobic. Sometimes things are done for the agoraphobic which removes the need for assuming responsibility. I am not saying this is the agoraphobics choice, but, because of the limitations of agoraphobia, they are usually not expected to do many things.

There is also the matter of relationships. A relationship, such as a marriage, can be based on one spouse being dependent and needy and the other fulfilling the role of protector and provider. As long as this arrangement is maintained, the marriage is secure. To some, this could justify remaining agoraphobic.

Another "payoff" is not being able to fulfill other people's expectations. By being limited, you do not have to face situations or events that you do not WANT to face. You have the perfect out. You are an agoraphobic.

There is also the fear of recovery. It is difficult to imagine what it would be like as a recovered person when you are limited by childlike fears. The fear of what is going to be expected of you if you are recovered can prevent recovery.

An example might be a housewife that knows she will be expected to go to work if she recovers. She is not lazy or inept. She would like to be in the outside world. However, she fantasizes about the travel to the job, being confined, the responsibility, being away from familiar surroundings, not having a support person close by, and, while she is limited as an active agoraphobic, these thoughts are extremely frightening. She has difficulty in accepting that if she follows the steps to recovery as outlined in this book, she will be well prepared to face these challenges and will not have the same feelings and attitudes she has while she is limited.

If there are "payoffs" in remaining agoraphobic, realize that *YOU DO NOT HAVE TO RECOVER!* That is a confusing statement and seems contradictory to the direction of this book. I have written about and encouraged recovery, and now I am saying that you do not have to recover. Let me explain:

If the limitations created by agoraphobia benefit you and do not cause hardship for those around you, you can spend your life as an agoraphobic, but, you do not have to suffer the pain, frustrations, anxiety and fears. You can go as far as you wish along the road to recovery, and then stop. What you do with your life is your choice. I have known many agoraphobics who have reached their levels of comfort and stopped there. Their life is fulfilling for them and they are happy. It depends on the circumstances, the interrelationships, and the hardships the limitations create.

I have worked with a homebound agoraphobic who created a very satisfying lifestyle for herself. She is a music teacher and her students come to her home. She feels she is a contributor to society by teaching young people to play the piano. A supportive family takes care of the outside needs and activities and she takes care of the home. She was content in her lifestyle and when she learned the techniques of controlling her anxieties, she stopped the process. She had what she wanted.

Another was married to a macho man. Their relationship was based on her dependency and his strength. In the process of recovery, she started to feel resentment on his part. She also felt resentful because he did not encourage her growth. A conflict developed and she came to realize that if she recovered, she might ruin her marriage. So, she went just far enough to do some of the things she wanted to do, comfortably. Again, this was her choice.

What recovery means differs from individual to individual. A twenty-one year old male might have different recovery goals than a fifty-five year old female. The man might want to get into a career, get married, travel, attain financial success and do all those things a "man" would do. The fifty-five year old woman, having already had her children and desiring to focus on being the wife and mother she would like to be, may consider recovery being able to go shopping alone, taking trips with her husband, being able to visit her children and generally living a peaceful, nonchallenging lifestyle. Both, when their goals are attained, have recovered.

No one else can dictate to you what your recovery should be. You are the only one who really knows. Agoraphobics understand more about the causes and conditions and recovery from agoraphobia than 95% of the psychologists and psychiatrists who are treating them.

In your recovering process, it would be beneficial to eliminate the label of agoraphobia. I have met many "recovered" agoraphobics who still consider themselves "phobic." They have been told that they would be this way the rest of their lives and they must learn to adapt to it. This is absolute nonsense. That attitude keeps a person limited, and we have proven many times at the New Beginning Foundation that they could be "unlimited."

If you decide to go for full recovery, then don't settle for anything less. It is attainable and achievable. I encourage agoraphobics who are on the road to recovery to think of themselves as *"NORMAL"* functional human beings, *DEALING* with some limitations." The key words are "normal" and "dealing." You are "normal" as I have previously explained, and are "dealing" with some limitations. It may come as a surprise to you, but most of the "civilian world" are "dealing" with some limitations. You are no different. You are working through your problems.

Be prepared for some confusion on the part of those close to you while you are recovering. They may not understand that the road has many turns and is not always smooth. They may feel that if you have a couple of successes you are recovered. Don't allow them to force you to do what you do not feel you are ready to do. You must be the judge.

There may also be resentment of the "new you." This is because they are not accustomed to you acting differently than you may have for years. Your higher levels of confidence and self worth will be challenging to them. Those closest to you might try to sabotage your growth. This is not necessarily intentional. It is just that they are feeling insecure and confused. Their roles might change and people resent change. You might find some friends that you had when needy and dependent no longer coming around. This is the time for you to be understanding and patient. Realize they feel threatened and do what you can to assure them that, even if you change, in many ways you are basically the same person.

During the process of recovering, you might find that you feel like a teenager again. You might want to do things that others would consider silly or inappropriate for you to do. This is a natural and normal part of your growth and your journey. It can become confusing to those around you. You might feel like a rebellious teenager. You resent others telling you what to do and reject authority figures. Do not become overly concerned. This is a temporary stage of your growth. It will pass and you will mature to the chronological age you are supposed to be. But, I must warn you, you will find many differences in yourself and realize you are not the same person you were before.

This is my definition of recovery. As I said at the beginning of this chapter, recovery can be simple or complex. I believe in K.I.S.S. (Keep It Simple, Stupid)

RECOVERY: When you no longer think of yourself as an agoraphobic.

There it is!!! Can you attain that goal? Thousands have. The road to recovery is well traveled, has rocks and stones, obstacles, turns, hills and valleys, fair weather and foul weather. It also has long distances that are smooth and level. All it takes is the first step to start the journey. Good luck!

Taking Charge of Your Life

19

The techniques already recommended to control anxiety, along with attitudes to help in the growth process, will eliminate much of the confusion and mystery of agoraphobia. One of the most important factors needed in traveling the road to recovery is taking responsibility for yourself. No one can make the trip for you. You may have help and support, but it is up to you to take the first step that starts the trip, and then to persevere towards your goal of being the person you want to be.

Typically, the road is not a smooth one. It has hills and valleys (good days and bad days), all kinds of obstacles (situations and events which challenge you) and many forks in the road (What do I do now?). You may doubt your ability to continue the trip (Is it worth the frustration?) and it has many curves (Am I still growing, or am I going backwards?). Despite this, go forward with confidence and faith that the road is leading you towards your destination.

Taking charge of your life means that you have certain rights and privileges and that these rights are yours to be used as a mature, independent person, rather than a limited child.

A recovered agoraphobic sent me the "Bill of Rights for Winners," which I would like to share with you:

You have the right to be you . . . the way you are . . . the way you want to be.

You have the right to grow, to change, to become, to strive, to reach for any goal, to be limited only by your degree of talent and amount of effort.

You have the right to privacy . . . in marriage, family or any relationship or group . . . the right to keep a part of your life secret, no matter how trivial or important, merely because you want it to be that way.

You have the right to be alone part of each day, each week and each year to spend time with and on yourself.

You have the right to be loved . . . and to love . . . to be accepted, cared for, and adored . . . and you have the right to fulfill that right.

You have the right to ask questions of anyone at anytime in any matter that affects your life, so long as it is your business to do so . . . and to be listened to and taken seriously.

You have the right to self respect and to do everything you need to do to increase your self esteem, so long as you hurt no one in doing so.

You have the right to be happy . . . to find something in the world that is meaningful and rewarding to you and that gives you a sense of completeness.

You have the right to be trusted . . . and to trust . . . and to be taken at your word. If you are wrong, you have the right to be given a chance to make good, if possible.

You have the right to be free as long as you act responsibly and are mindful of the rights of others and of those obligations that you entered into freely.

You have the right to win . . . to succeed . . . to make plans and to see those plans fulfilled . . . to become the best you can possibly become.

I would like to add that as an agoraphobic:

You have the right to be accepted . . .

To ask for support when needed . . .

To deal with your everyday life as best you can . . .

To back off when you need to . . .

And the right to say NO!

Only you can set the pace for your growth. Others not walking in your shoes do not know how difficult the trip to recovery is. "Should's, have to's and ought to's" coming from others are obstacles on the road and have to be dealt with. Only you can determine how far you want to travel at any given time. It is your responsibility to plan the route and to set the speed under which you are going to travel.

CASE HISTORY—SARAH

I would like you to meet Sarah, a young lady who came to me through her psychologist's recommendation. She had come to a standstill in her ability to get past her agoraphobia. Her self doubt and old insecurities kept her from progressing in her recovery. She had a supportive husband who was frustrated and confused by his inability to help her. Sarah began the New Beginning "At Home" program and we started our ongoing telephone consultation procedures. I was "Uncle Mel" to her and our relationship became a warm and sharing one.

At first she resisted changes that were starting to take place. She was in conflict between her old fears and the new attitudes that were becoming part of her belief system. Soon, with the proper support, from both her husband and myself, she started to take some small risks. With her successes, she developed self confidence. The more confident she felt, the larger the risks she was willing to take on. She finally accepted the responsibility of her own growth and recovery.

Last Christmas I received the following letter from Sarah. I would like to share it with you . . .

Dear Mel:

I thought I would write to you and let you know how wonderful my life is! There is so much to say, I don't know where to begin. To start with, let me tell you this once "housebound agoraphobic" is now the office manager, working forty and more hours per week. I get all the wonderful headaches and responsibilities that go with being a manager, and, of course, I love it.

I am still attending college part time in the evenings. Once I graduate I plan on attending a four year university. I am majoring in social and behavioral sciences. It is a wonder how much one learns about life by furthering the education.

Life has become such a challenge to me. There is so much to do, and believe me, I plan on doing it all. I have become so much stronger in these last few years than I ever was before. I can't believe I'm the same person. I have control over my life, and it feels wonderful. I have, what I call "come to terms" with a lot of my emotions. I have established what in life is important to me.

Last Thursday my husband Mort and I attended a friend's funeral. I was really dreading it. Pat, the woman who died, was a friend I had worked with for years. She became disabled last July and passed away last Sunday. She had died from cancer. I knew in my heart she would never recover and would eventually die. I often wondered how I would handle it, once she did. I thought I would break down. But, you know what? I didn't. I handled it. And the funeral that I dreaded so much, I handled that too. I was even glad I attended the funeral. I learned something very important from that experience. I learned it was O.K. to die. That dying is something that one day we all must face. Sounds pretty calm coming from a person who had a dreaded fear of death.

On to better news. Mort and I are planning a trip to Hawaii in 1985. I can't wait! It will be my first experience on a large plane, and a first for being that far away from home. I know we will have a great time.

Of course, I do want to mention that none of this would have been possible without you and New Beginning. Thanks to your "At Home" program and all our wonderful phone calls, I feel like a real person. I feel great about the person I am and the life I am living. Again, Uncle Mel, thank you so much for all of your help in the past. Couldn't have done it without you.

Love,
Sarah

Sarah is typical of a former agoraphobic who has gone forward on the road to recovery. She took the ball and ran with it. She used what she learned and took the risks necessary for her growth. I am not responsible for Sarah's life as she is experiencing it now. Only she is. She "took charge of her life" and is attaining her goals.

Living a worthwhile life is the same for everyone, not only agoraphobics. We all have to learn to make adjustments. In my lectures on agoraphobia, I have stated that "the only difference between me and a bum on skid row, is how I adjusted to the negatives of life." His adjustment was a wine bottle, mine was to deal with the negatives in another way. We both had to adjust.

The ability to adjust is not a God given gift. It is learned. Most ways of adjusting are learned early in life. Problems arise when we do not learn to change, when the adjustments we are making are not working for us. We keep using the "tried and true" even though the results are not satisfactory. We keep making the same mistakes because to make a change calls for risk. Then, we wonder why things do not work out for us. If we reflect upon past history, we would realize that in making the same adjustments, we always end up with the same negative results.

There is a risk involved when we make changes in our lives. One thing we should be prepared for is the opposition we are going to receive from those around us. You see, there is a law in physics that states "for every action, there is a reaction." This is also true of life. Your change demands that other persons change also. They have to "adjust" to the new you. They may resent this, since they also have to take a risk. They may sincerely want you to change, but they do not want the change to affect them. Be aware of their problems and insecurities in dealing with a different person than the one they have been accustomed to for many years. Make them feel more secure by reassuring them that the "new you" is not a threat to them. Tell them how the positive changes will benefit them and that by accepting the "new you" their lives will also be better.

Sometimes, others push hot buttons that can change our attitudes about what we are trying to accomplish. They use words that can recreate our old feelings of insecurity. Words such as don't . . . ought . . . should . . . always . . . never . . . must. These are known as parent words. When we cannot fulfill the goal set by the word, we feel guilt and insecurity. Examples are:

You *don't* ever want to go anywhere.

You *ought* to be able to do that.

156

You *should* not be afraid to be alone.

You *always* have problems.

You *never* feel well.

You *must* force yourself to do it.

Any one of these words, when used by others, may create the feelings of being trapped. This is because someone else is setting goals for us and they are not our goals. These parent words are very manipulative. They push the same hot buttons that were pushed when we were children. Other manipulative words are selfish . . . don't care . . . hurting me . . . make me angry . . . and so on. When others try to set our goals (usually for their benefit, not ours) they will use these words and feel that we must react.

I would like to add a new word to your vocabulary, one I learned from Zig Zigler. This word will prevent you from reacting, unless it is to your benefit. The word is SNIOP. It sounds like a nonsense word, doesn't it? There is no such word, is there? Well, there should be. SNIOP stands for:

S — *S*uggestible or *s*usceptible to the
N — *N*egative
I — *I*nfluences of
O — *O*ther
P — *P*eople

There it is. If you feel the message coming down to you of "should . . . ought or must," immediately say to yourself, "I am being *SNIOP'ed*." You are becoming *S*uggestible or *S*usceptible to the *N*egative *I*nfluences of *O*ther *P*eople. Realize that this is taking place, reflect on the situation and act (not react) accordingly. Rmember, you can only be manipulated if you allow it to happen. Learn to stand your ground, tell yourself "I am not a child. I will not be SNIOP'ed." There is power in words. They can be used for your benefit or against you. Use them to help you.

When we start to take charge of our lives, there is a tendency to want to make all of the changes at one time and to go from one end of the spectrum to the other in one move. Remember, the ability to adjust and change is learned, and like all learning experiences, takes time. You did not learn to ride a bike by just getting on it and peddling. You had to learn balance, timing and perception. And, most importantly, you had to practice. Determine how and what you want to change in your life and plan your attack. Use any techniques and tools available to you. Use others support and advice, when necessary. Do everything you can to make the adjustment a successful one. If you have a failure, do not stop in your venture. Start again, and make an adjustment so that you do not repeat the circumstances that led to the failure.

This next statement may not seem to be important, but in my recovery, I found it to be very important. Develop a sense of humor about yourself and your situation. Do not take life too seriously. If you can laugh at yourself and your circumstances, you will realize that it is all a "game." It has been referred to as "the game of life." Being responsible and playing the "game of life" is not contradictory. Games have rules and the rules are to be followed. There are winners and losers. Some play the game better than others because they have learned to adjust and have practiced playing.

A technique I used during my recovery was to collect sayings and to put them on a bulletin board near my desk. Some of my favorite are:

It takes little courage to repeat yesterday.

The only way to change is to start.

Make your goals more important than your temptations.

There is no end to education.

Failure is a learning experience.

Being dependent for approval on anyone else is like expecting them to know where you itch and how to scratch it.

When you play your own game, people you like will join your team.

Most of our dreams of happiness in the future can be fulfilled by savoring the moment.

If you can't change it or accept it, then forget it.

Those brave enough to risk never regret what might have been.

If you cannot fight and cannot flee . . . then flow.

I could go on and on. I surrounded myself with positive ideas and thoughts. They all became part of my new belief system. They helped me put things into perspective.

Other sayings were humorous and allowed me to laugh at the peculiarities of life. I have often thought that whatever eternal powers there may be, he (or she) has a wonderful sense of humor. Some of my favorites are . . .

If there is a possibility of several things going wrong, the one that will cause the most damage will be the one to go wrong.

Anytime things seem to be going better, you've over looked something.

Nothing is impossible for a man who doesn't have to do it himself.

Once a job is fouled up, anything done to improve it makes it worse.

There's never enough time to do it right, but there's always enough time to do it over.

You cannot determine beforehand which side of the bread to butter.

A chicken does not stop scratching just because the worms are scarce.

No matter where you go . . . there you are.

When the going gets tough . . . everyone leaves.

If the shoe fits . . . it's ugly.

Even rats scurrying on a treadmill have the feeling they're going somewhere.

And my favorite which I attribute to my uncle: Prohibition was better than no alcohol at all.

And so I learned, as you will, that it's all in the way you look at life and how you adjust. How I chose to live my life was my responsibility, and no one else's. I had to take the risks necessary for growth and fought the battle daily. I won some and lost some, but I went forward. It takes courage, which every agoraphobic possesses. I sometimes lost faith in myself, but it was always temporary. I felt sorry for myself at times and wondered if it was all worth it. I was encouraged and discouraged by others. I felt anxiety and panic, and I felt a sense of calmness. I felt scared and I felt confident. I felt negative and I felt positive. The road had obstacles and I had to decide whether to go under them, around them or over them . . . or perhaps . . . just sit quietly and stare at them for a while. I learned and I practiced what I learned.

I only knew one thing for sure . . . and that was that I was put on the earth for a purpose and that purpose was going to be fulfilled. By writing this book, I feel it was.

Kathy's Story—From Homebound to Recovery

20

It was a typical day in the high desert of Southern California. The sun was shining brightly and the air was clear. Kathy put her two year old son in the Pinto to do the weekly shopping at the local super-market. It was the same every week . . . a trip to the super-market, then stopping for a treat at Baskin-Robbins for her son, and back home in time for "Days Of Our Lives."

Shea ran ahead of her into the supermarket when they arrived and chose the basket he wanted to ride in. She picked him up and put him in the kiddy seat. Walking the aisles, she checked her selections against her shopping list.

Suddenly, she felt as if a shroud fell over her. Her legs became weak and she had to hold on to the shelving for support. Her heart was pounding in her chest and things around her went out of focus. She felt very cold and clammy at the same time. She couldn't breath properly and felt like she was going to choke. She had a sinking sensation in the bottom of her stomach, and then a rush from her stomach to her chest. She was lightheaded and dizzy and was sure she was going to faint. She had to get out of there.

She held on to the shopping cart for balance and rushed to the check out counter. Only sheer willpower kept her from leaving the groceries and fleeing outside. The store was spinning around her, but she held on. It seemed like the clerk was taking forever in checking out the people in front of her. Finally it was her turn. Everything seemed cloudy and unreal, as if she were in a bad dream. She was sure everyone could hear her pounding heartbeat. The clerk said something to her. She stared at him and tried to listen as he was telling her the amount of her purchase. Shakily, she reached into her purse and took out her checkbook and pen. She started to write and her hand shook so badly, she pressed harder on the pen. What seemed like an eternity passed as she wrote the check. Her groceries were placed in a cart and she ran for the door. When she got to the car, she realized that Shea was not with her. In her panicky state, she forgot about him. She went towards the store again, and Shea was outside, confused. She took his hand and hurried to the car.

When she sat behind the wheel, she took a deep breath and started to feel better. Her heartbeat was slowing and things came back into focus. She sat for a moment before turning the ignition key. She looked around her. Everything was returning to normal, but she had a tight knot in her stomach.

She drove home slowly, still a little shaken. When she arrived, she left the groceries in the car and headed for the kitchen. She reached into the cabinet and brought forth a bottle of wine. She poured a little into a glass and swallowed it quickly. A feeling of warmth passed over her and she felt better. She left the bottle on the counter and took her groceries out of the car. She had another drink while putting them away. Everything was fine now.

She was concerned about what had happened. "It must be the flu or a virus," she thought. She would take it easy for the next couple of days. She put Shea in his room and settled down for her soap opera, with a drink in her hand. All is well with the world again.

A week passed uneventfully. She did her household chores, took care of the family needs and followed her usual routine. It was time to do the shopping again. There was a little knot in her stomach when she drove to the supermarket. As she parked the car and started to walk to the entrance, the feeling grew and she began to feel fearful, of what she did not know. When she entered the store, she hesitated. The lights seemed very bright. She took a basket and headed for the aisles. The further she went into the store, the more nervous she felt. "This is crazy," she thought. She pushed herself further, and as she did so, she started to feel weaker and weaker. Her heart started to pound again. The store spun around her. The fear turned into a feeling of impending doom. She could not stay there. Leaving the groceries, she rushed for the exit, pushing her way through the check out line and into the sunshine. She got into the car and rushed home. She was still frightened and her heart was beating hard. She immediately went to the liquor cabinet and poured herself a drink. Soon she felt calmer, but she was scared. This second time was worse than the first. "What is happening?" she asked herself. After two drinks, she felt better, but very confused.

That night she told her husband what had happened. He did not take it seriously, but suggested that she take it easy. They were having some financial difficulties and maybe she was worrying too much. He assured her that everything would be all right. She slept fitfully that night. That funny feeling in her stomach was concerning her. Her mind seemed to be in a jumble and she felt frightened. She got up many times during the night and sat smoking in the living room. She tried to sort out her feelings. The more she tried, the more fearful she became. She made up her mind to see her doctor. Perhaps there was a flu going around and she had caught it.

The next morning she called and made an appointment with her doctor. Driving to his office she thought, "This is crazy. What am I going to tell him? I feel fine now. I'll just be taking up his time." When she arrived, she smoked a cigarette in the car and pulled her thoughts together. When the doctor saw her, she told him what had happened but did not make it seem important. She didn't want him to think that she was taking it seriously. "Just something I wanted checked out," she said. He checked her vital signs and everything was normal. "You're probably under a little pressure," he said. He prescribed Valium to be taken as needed and assured her that everything was OK.

When she was driving home, she had to make a left turn to get on to the street leading to her house. The traffic was heavy and she was surrounded by cars. Her accelerator foot started to tremble and she suddenly felt the fear she had experienced in the supermarket. She felt trapped in her car waiting to make the left turn. She put the car in neutral gear and started to shake. "Move, damn you . . . move," she shouted in her mind. Finally, after what seemed like an eternity, she made the turn and rushed home. She lay down on the couch, breathing heavily. Her body was shaking badly and she was frightened. "What is going on?," she thought.

That night, she and the family went out for dinner. They were sitting in their favorite Mexican restaurant and dinner was ordered. In the middle of dinner, the feelings hit her again. The room started to spin and she felt the shroud fall over her again. She stood up and said "We have to leave right now." The children and her husband looked at her like she was a madwoman. She was white and shaking. Her husband asked what was wrong. She did not answer, but rushed for the door. Once outside, she leaned against the car, gasping for breath. Her husband and children followed and they went home in silence. She went to bed.

She spent the next few days at home, avoiding neighbors and outside trips. She was not herself, and the children and her husband were confused. She didn't talk much and went to bed right after the dishes were done. Her husband did the weekly shopping. She started to spend her days cleaning and then re-cleaning the house. She vacuumed every day, sometimes twice a day. She could not sit still. The Valium did not seem to help. The only time she felt some sense of calmness was when she had a drink. She was drinking more than usual.

When she tried to leave her home alone, she felt nervous just crossing her threshold. She did not drive, remembering what she experienced making the left turn. Days passed and she did not venture outside. She was becoming withdrawn. The fear within her was growing and she was in a constant daze. She spent a lot of time in bed, waiting for her older son to come home from school. She felt better not being alone. She asked him not to go to far "because she may need him to do some chores." She prepared dinner while he was home and had a drink before her husband arrived.

Everyone was walking on eggshells around her. Her husband took care of the two year old after work and on weekends. Kathy was drinking more and more, and he could not stop her. She slept a lot and was getting sloppy in her appearance. She didn't seem to care about herself or anyone else. When he tried to speak to her, she stared at him and cried. He started to believe she was going crazy. He urged her to see another doctor. She told him she was frightened. "What if I am crazy? They will put me away." Another thought, perhaps one that was more important, was that the doctor might take away the liquor. That was her only relief from the feelings that caused the panic. No . . . she would not see another doctor. "It will pass," she assured him. "Be patient and don't push me."

Kathy became virtually a prisoner in her own home. The only time she went out was with her husband, and then well fortified with liquor. The days became months and then years. There were times she felt the fear at home, but her old friend, the alcohol, was close by. The family adjusted to her condition, and her husband stopped pushing her to see a doctor. Kathy had become a homebound agoraphobic.

What led up to this? Why would a normal housewife, active and apparently happy, become a fearful, limited person, dependant on alcohol to complete the simplest chores.

Kathy was 32 years old when she experienced her first panic in the supermarket. The family had moved to the desert because of her husbands work. She had left her own job when her youngest son was born. It was the first time she was a full time housewife. She was also lonely in her new environment. The family was having financial troubles, and she worried about that. Her husband worked odd shifts, and she was left alone a lot. Her oldest son was going through his early teenage years and was a concern to her. Her old friends were left behind when they moved to the desert and her parents retired to Florida. There she was, in a strange town, without friends, without the secure schedule of a working wife, which she followed for years, not getting satisfaction from her role of housewife, losing her sense of self worth and accomplishment, worried about the finances and her children, and, she became subconsciously overwhelmed.

When this happened, she regressed back to her childhood belief system. She was brought up in Upstate New York. She had a brother who her father adored and she was jealous of him. She wished she were an only child so that her father would play with her like he did with her brother. Her mother was critical of her, always putting her down. Her father was more supportive, but fearful of his wife's criticism. When she was 5 years old, her brother contracted polio and died. She felt sure that she caused his death because of her wishes to be the loved child. After her brother's death, her parents never spoke about him. It was like he did not exist. Kathy and her mother became competitors for her fathers attention and her mother became even more critical of her. She felt very unloved and insecure.

By the time she was 12 years old, she weighed 175 pounds. The other children made fun of her and she became a "loner". The friends she gravitated to shared her feelings of insecurity and inadequacy. Her father and mother both worked, so she spent a lot of time by herself. She would fantasize that she was beautiful and loved by all. She and her best friend would play a game of "What it would be like if their parents died and they had all the money and freedom they wanted."

She was a compliant student and tried to please her teachers. She got into trouble only once, and that devastated her. She felt her teacher did not like her. As a matter of fact, she was sure that no one liked her, especially her father. She tried and tried to please him, but her efforts were ignored. Her mother was better, but it was her father that she longed to satisfy.

During high school, she went on a strict diet and lost weight. She joined the school glee club and was branching out. She made friends and started dating. Her high school years were her fondest memories. She was *almost* like the other kids. Still, she felt a little different.

Her first husband was her high school sweetheart. He was on the football team and she was flattered that she had attracted him. He joined the Navy after he graduated high school and they were married. He had a dominant personality and Kathy was the passive, dependent wife. When he was transferred to Hawaii, she joined him. Soon, their son was born. She was left alone a lot because of his sea duty. Her first son was not a well child and she felt nervous when he was ill. Her husband drank a lot when he was at home and became abusive. He beat her on occasion and told her she was stupid and lazy. As she did with her father, she tried to win his love. As it was with her father, she was rejected.

When they returned stateside, her husband left her. He filed for divorce and she did not protest. She became a single mother without training or skills. She had to find a job and eventually she learned to be a keypunch operator. Refusing to go home to her parents, she moved from city to city with her son, trying to find someplace she felt she could call home. She met her present husband in a bar in Atlanta, Georgia. He seemed nice and liked her son. He pursued her and they were married, moving to Northern California, near his parents. His mother watched her son, and Kathy returned to work. Their second son was born and she stayed home with him. Everything went well until he was transferred to Southern California and the desert. It seemed to be a good opportunity and Kathy wanted to get away from his parents. Six months later, Kathy was a homebound agoraphobic.

For the entire 5 years she was homebound, Kathy did not know that she was agoraphobic. She sometimes thought she was crazy, but knew deep down that she wasn't. Everyday she prayed that she would be "normal" again. She kept her house in order, feeling that if her house was in order, her life would also be in order. All of the canned goods in her cabinet were in alphabetical order and she became hysterical if someone moved a can. If there was a piece of lint on the living room carpet, she would vacuum the entire room. It was she and the alcohol against the world. No one understood and no one cared, she thought.

One morning, watching television, she saw a program on which a doctor was describing agoraphobia. She sat glued to the spot and did not believe what she was hearing. He was describing her. There was a name for her affliction. She woke her husband, tears running down her face. "I'm not crazy," she shouted. "There's a name for me. I'm agoraphobic." He looked at her as if she finally flipped out. She was pacing the room, talking out loud. "If there's a name, there's help. Other people have the same thing I have and get better. That's what the doctor said." The next day she called her own doctor, telling him what she saw on television. He told her he didn't know anything about agoraphobia and she should see a psychiatrist. That posed two problems. One was getting to a psychiatrist since leaving home was too fearful and second was her dread of having to give up the alcohol. She was not aware that she had become alcoholic as well as agoraphobic.

Upon her husbands insistence, she called her doctor back and he recommended a psychiatrist. With her husband at her side and fortified with alcohol and Valium, she went to her first appointment. The psychiatrist found it difficult to understand her being homebound for 5 years. He told her there were deep seated problems to work on and it might take years before they had answers. In the meanwhile, he prescribed other medication. She did not tell him about her drinking habits.

She continued being treated by him for a year. During that time she did not have any relief from her anxiety, except to dull it with the use of alcohol. She drank vodka when she had her appointment so that her doctor would not smell it. She only went out with her husband and then to "safe" and well known places. She still had the anticipatory fears, never knowing when a panic attack would strike again. She was not getting better.

One day her husband pointed out an article in the local newspaper. It announced that a support group for agoraphobics was forming in the town next to theirs. He asked her to call for more information and she said she would. But, the fear of the unknown was strong within her. "What would a group be like? I'm probably worse than anyone else. They will think I am crazy. What if they tell me I can't drink? Who are these people from the New Beginning Foundation that are running the group? I never heard of them."

She avoided the call for two weeks, telling her husband the line was always busy. Finally he called, and got the necessary information. He told her they were going to a meeting that week. She did not sleep well the night before the meeting. She was nervous and scared. The next town was 9 miles away and she had not been that far from home for 5 years.

She started drinking the afternoon of the day of the meeting. Vodka, of course. That night she could not eat dinner and tried to tell her husband she did not feel well. He insisted they go to the meeting and she went with great apprehension.

She did not say a word on the trip over to the next town. She was trying to control her fears, and the more she tried, the worse they became. She told her husband to turn back, but he would not. She cried silently until they finally arrived.

As she entered the home where the meeting was being held, she was surprised by the number of people who were there. They all seemed so "normal." "Probably none of them are as bad as I am," she thought. She found a seat near the door and told her husband that she was not going to stay for the entire meeting. She was too nervous. He put his arm around her and they waited for the meeting to begin.

I was the leader of that meeting. There were approximately 15 agoraphobics present with their support persons. They all sat silently and stared at me. I started by telling of my personal experiences as an agoraphobic, and asking, "Does that sound familiar?" everytime I told of a limitation or fear. Soon I saw their heads nodding affirmatively as I was speaking. I asked for questions, and the group started to inter-act. I particularly noted Kathy sitting in a dark corner, smoking constantly and I sensed her tension. I asked her if she wanted to share her experiences, and she just shook her head "no." "She will not be back," I told myself.

We set up an ongoing schedule of weekly meetings, to augment the New Beginning "At Home" program for recovery. Everyone agreed, but I knew from previous experience that only half would return the next week. In my mind I thought, "Kathy would be one that would not return."

Much to my surprise, she did come the next week. We discussed agoraphobia and I encouraged everyone to share experiences and feelings. Kathy did not participate that second week, but did the third. She told of her confusion and fear about going crazy, and was encouraged when the others in the group shared that they felt the same. I thanked her for speaking after the meeting, and she smiled.

The next month, Kathy shared more during the meetings. She became more comfortable with the group and was keeping in touch with some of the members outside of the meetings by telephone. I introduced the first set of programmed cassettes to the group and I remember Kathy's excitement about receiving them.

It was time for the group to work on their own with the programmed cassettes. I told them I would be available by telephone if they needed me and to use the cassettes as instructed. I heard from various members of the original group, but not Kathy. Being involved with many other agoraphobics, I did not think of her, until one morning, six months later, she called. She was very excited.

Her son was returning by bus from a trip to his grandmother in Northern California and the bus stop was 30 miles from their home. Her husband was going to pick him up, but then he was assigned a double shift that day and could not do it. Their son would just have to wait at the bus stop until he could get him and that might be six hours.

Kathy had been playing her tapes faithfully and began practicing going out on her own. She found that she could control her feelings of anxiety with the process and that gave her the confidence to take a few small risks. She

167

was feeling better about herself and felt, for the first time in five long years, that she could be "normal" again. She started driving around town, and doing some shopping in small stores. I often mention in the programmed cassettes that you do not have to create challenges to test yourself. Life will create the challenges for you. Kathy felt that her son's arrival was that type of challenge and believed she was ready.

She called me after she picked up her son. She told me of the nervousness she felt when she made the commitment to do it to herself. She decided that she would not do it with the aid of alcohol. However, she would have a flask in the trunk of the car, "just in case." She made the trip one mile at a time, knowing that she could turn back at any time. As she passed the half way mark (15 miles) she could not believe how calm she was. She put her foot on the gas and continued forward. When she arrived at the bus stop, her son was waiting. He saw her behind the wheel and he approached the car and looked in the back seat. He thought his father was hiding there and it was a joke. When he realized that his mother had made the trip by herself, he started to laugh and soon they were laughing together. On the trip back, Kathy was singing and smiling. She did not want to stop. She wanted to keep driving forever. She felt a sense of freedom that she had not felt for years.

From that point on, Kathy called me weekly. She had her good days and bad days, but she persevered. She played her tapes and took her risks. She felt her fears, and overcame them. She substituted "So What!" for "What if?" One year from our initial meeting, Kathy announced that she was recovered. She was working part time and joined Alcoholics Anonymous to deal with her drinking problem.

Three months later, we needed a secretary in our offices in North Hollywood. My associate at the time suggested Kathy as a possibility. I was concerned because of the 120 mile commute she would have daily to and from work. However, I had my associate call her and offer her the position. Much to my surprise, she accepted it. The next week, Kathy started work at the New Beginning Foundation.

Three years have passed since that day. Kathy is now Director or Counselling and my right arm. She has led support groups, counseled hundreds of agoraphobics, traveled to far away cities, been on television and radio, and still drives that 120 miles by herself. She has become involved with her A.A. program and has helped others in that direction.

Kathy was a classic agoraphobic. Her childhood programming led her to become agoraphobic. Her adjustment to her limitations, her fears and frustration are no different than yours. She is not an exception. We have helped hundreds of agoraphobics become as unlimited as she is. Recovery is not only achievable, but definitely possible with the proper therapy and a desire to recover. Do not give up. Find what will work for you and stick to it. I wish for you what I wish for all agoraphobics . . . freedom, peace of mind and a fulfilling life.

God bless you.

The New Beginning Foundation

Incorporated in 1980 as a public/charitable organization the New Beginning Foundation based in North Hollywood, California is the nations only non-profit organization established to help the victims of agoraphobia attain recovery and to provide information to the professional community and general public concerning this problem.

Melvin D. Green, a recovered agoraphobic, author and lecturer, is the Founding Director.

After years of research, the Foundation has developed the New Beginning "Fear Free" program which has proven to be extremely effective in helping agoraphobics attain recovery.

The "Fear Free" program can be used by sufferers of agoraphobia anywhere in the English speaking world in the safety of their own homes. It is a step-by-step building block program utilizing audio cassettes and ongoing telephone consultation.

New Beginning Foundation can be contacted by writing:

NEW BEGINNING FOUNDATION
P.O. BOX 15519
NORTH HOLLYWOOD, CALIFORNIA 91615–15519

Cross Index